Oil Lamps II

Glass Kerosene Lamps

CATHERINE M. V. THURO

Also by Catherine M. V. Thuro
OIL LAMPS
The Kerosene Era in North America
PRIMITIVES & FOLK ART
Our Handmade Heritage
Designed and Produced by Catherine M. V. Thuro
The Marketplace Guide to
OAK FURNITURE Styles & Values
by Peter S. Blundell
The Marketplace Guide to
VICTORIAN FURNITURE Styles & Values
by Peter S. Blundell and Phil T. Dunning

Oil Lamps II

Glass Kerosene Lamps

ISBN 0-89145-226-5

Photography and Design by Catherine M. V. Thuro
Staff Artist, John R. Wright
Typeset in Oracle by Canada Stamp/Graphics
Color separations by Praven Graphic Productions Inc.
Printed and bound in Canada by The Bryant Press Ltd.

Cover Photograph, Lamps described on p. 97

Published by

Thorncliffe House Inc.
4 William Morgan Dr., Thorncliffe Park
Toronto, ON M4H 1E6

Published simultaneously in the United States and Distributed by

Collector Books
Box 3009
Paducah, KY 42001

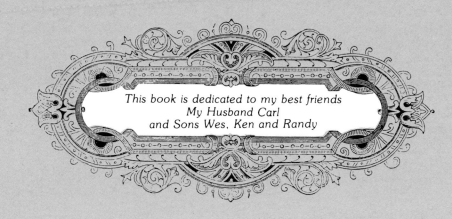

This book is dedicated to my best friends
My Husband Carl
and Sons Wes, Ken and Randy

Foreword

For over two thousand years, from before the birth of Christ until the late eighteenth century, there was little progress in the development of lighting. Grease lamps used in Greece and Rome in the second century B.C. differ only in appearance from those still being used in Pennsylvania and other parts of America well into the middle of the nineteenth century. Francois Aimé Argand's invention in 1784 of the tubular wick and the principles embodied in the Argand lamp and Miles's patent agitable lamp foreshadowed other experiments and improvements in lighting that followed in the first half of the nineteenth century. Among them were the development of gas lighting, the expanded use of whale oil for lamp fuel and the invention of the brighter, but highly volatile and extremely dangerous, burning fluids.

But it was coal oil, or kerosene, as it was called by Dr. Abraham Gesner, a Canadian geologist who patented his discovery in the United States in 1854, coupled with the drilling of the first oil well in Pennsylvania in 1859 that was the first major break-through in the history of lighting. Its abundance made it cheap and affordable to most of the population, and it was immediately adopted over widespread areas for use in homes, factories, public buildings, railroads and boats. Although kerosene lighting may seem to us today to be both romantic and inconvenient, it was then welcomed as a more convenient, brighter and safer form of lighting than any theretofore generally available. Its use extended the day as never before, and kerosene lighting devices were in great demand.

A myriad of types and forms of kerosene lamps — stand, hanging, and bracket, as well as lanterns — were quickly developed, and along with them, many diverse types of burners and chimneys. As the century progressed, kerosene lamps, which were usually decorative as well as practical, were affected by changing styles and tastes. This great demand continued throughout the nineteenth century, and even after the introduction of the electric lamp, kerosene was the usual form of illumination in rural areas until the 1930's. The impact of kerosene created new business for metal working and, especially, glass factories. The result was a tremendous range of kerosene lamps, many of which are still available to collectors today.

Despite an ever growing and widespread interest in collecting antiques, and a proliferation of books on collecting, there was no significant publication about kerosene lighting until 1976, when Catherine M. V. Thuro authored *Oil Lamps —The Kerosene Era in North America*. This landmark publication and basic text about the subject is now admirably complemented by Ms. Thuro's *Oil Lamps II — Glass Kerosene Lamps*.

Containing over 900 lamps, with more than 400 illustrated in color, this book details not only the development of the kerosene lamp and its changing styles, but also the wide variety produced during each of its different periods. Different types of glass, such as opal and alabaster in widespread use for lamp bases and fonts by nineteenth-century glassmakers, are discussed and distinguished by the author and related to contemporary formulae or receipts. Of special significance and importance is her discussion of the nomenclature of kerosene lamps and techniques of glass manufacture. All of this should be equally helpful to both lamp and glass collectors, since it clarifies many unrecognized techniques and much misunderstood terminology. Of further assistance and clarification is her introduction of the symbol[ON] to indicate the original name or number assigned to a lamp by the manufacturer, when known. Through painstakingly careful observation and meticulous research, she also has been able to relate numerous unmarked or otherwise unidentified lamps to marked or illustrated ones to arrive at numerous attributions by relationship. She terms this process, "sequential attribution", and it is an important one.

All of these factors, combined with a scrupulous desire for accuracy based upon detailed and documented research, plus the superb photographs she has taken for the entire book, provide a wealth of reliable information, as well as a visual treat for the lamp collector, glass collector and layperson, or casual collector, as well. Lamp collectors, who generally do not collect other glass, and glass collectors, who generally do not collect lamps, can benefit equally from this publication.

Kenneth M. Wilson,
Director of Collections and Preservation
Henry Ford Museum
Dearborn, Michigan

Introduction

"Between the dark and the daylight".

Longfellow's introductory line to his famous poem *The Children's Hour*, published in 1865, is an apt analogy to the role of the kerosene era in the history of lighting. The "dark" representing the meagre light of pre-kerosene lamps and candles; and the "daylight" approximated by electric lighting. The kerosene lamp provided ample inexpensive illumination for the majority of North American homes from its introduction in the late 1850's until its displacement by electric light beginning in the 1880's. New lamp designs were still being introduced in the 1930's to appeal to a rural population not yet reached by the distribution of electricity.

Recording this period requires the study of all pertinent material extant and relating it to primary source material. The aim of this book is to add to the stockpile of recorded information. It is intended for all who have an interest in the subject. The awareness, the heartwarming encouragement and the almost overwhelming co-operation and generosity of those who share my concern for all aspects of the subject, has led me to consider these friends as fellow students and researchers. Most of them may also be described as collectors, museum personnel or dealers; but the search for knowledge is the common denominator. Kerosene lighting is an exciting subject that has great potential for researchers. In time the magic of the open flame will obscure the pragmatic aspects remembered by those who have lived with it.

We will be left with a romantic image of the mellow light. I pick up my grade six reader with its pencilled tick mark beside the poem and continue to read, pausing to enjoy the picture suggested by the verse:

"From my study I see in the lamplight,
Descending the broad hall stair,
Grave Alice and laughing Allegra,
And Edith with golden hair."

Acknowledgements

Much of this book reflects the interest, expertise and generosity of the individuals whom I have consulted on a regular basis over the years. In listing their names (alphabetically) I wish to acknowledge their contribution and to extend my sincere thanks.

The following glass experts helped to guide my understanding of the subject and brought to my attention obscure and unpublished material.

G. Eason Eige, Chief Curator, Huntington, Galleries, Huntington, WV. The combination of Eason's artistic talents and knowledge of glass, has led to the success of the numerous glass exhibits he has formulated. This background coupled with his vision and enthusiasm was responsible for his overwhelming achievement: *The Great North American Kerosene Lamp Exhibit and Forum*. Brilliant design and scholarship were evident in the presentation of over 1100 lamps and accessories from our collection. Throughout the preparation for this event, Eason regularly provided valuable information, particularly with regard to Midwest glass.

Frank M. Fenton, Chairman of the Board of The Fenton Art Glass Company, has a family background with over eighty years of glassmaking. He shared not only his expertise in that area, but the knowledge and the accumulated data from his years of historical research relating to glassmaking in the Ohio Valley. My tour of their factory and visits to the company glass museum were rewarding experiences.

Peter Kaellgren, Curatorial Fellow in the European Department of the Royal Ontario Museum. In 1977 Peter organized the major exhibit *A Gather of Glass* at the ROM. He is currently completing a Ph.D. in Art History at the University of Delaware. For years Peter has shared his knowledge of glass; and more recently, when I decided to include foreign lamps, his knowledge of European decorative arts.

Kenneth M. Wilson, Director of Collections and Preservation, The Henry Ford Museum, Dearborn, MI. He is the author of *New England Glass and Glassmaking* and an internationally recognized authority on American glass. He is currently working on a general book on glass for the Henry Ford Museum, based on its collections; and a catalogue of the American glass in the Toledo Museum of Art. A continual flow of information, lively discussion and Ken's constructive criticism of my manuscript, have contributed significantly to the scope and accuracy of this work.

Speakers at the Forum held in conjunction with *The Great North American Kerosene Lamp Exhibit* have all had a bearing on this book. Some are mentioned elsewhere in the acknowledgements. Listed in the order they appear on the programme, they are:

Dr. Loris S. Russell. Fourteen years ago I purchased a pair of kerosene lamps from dealers Peter and Marion Blundell and was shown a copy of Dr. Russell's book, *A heritage of light: Lamps and lighting in the early Canadian home*. This landmark publication was the source of my inspiration to pursue the study of the kerosene era. The next discovery was learning the Russells lived in the same neighborhood. We have since spent many enjoyable evenings with Grace and Loris Russell.

Kenneth M. Wilson. Visits with Alice and Ken Wilson are somewhat curtailed by distance but supplemented by *frequent* telephone calls.

Jack A. Washka. Many of the lamps photographed for this book are from the outstanding collection of Emma Jo and Jack Washka. Their help and hospitality made our visits memorable.

Dr. Harry W. Rapp, Jr. The many Rushlight Club publications Harry has been involved with have been valuable references for both of my Oil Lamps books. We always enjoy our visits with Bette and Harry at the Rushlight Club meetings.

G. Eason Eige. The reality of the Lamp Exhibit he proposed, exceeded my most optimistic expectations.

Anne Marie Serio. The most fruitful outcome of my visits to the Smithsonian is the publication (in 1984) of a valuable 1889 kerosene lamp catalogue proposed jointly by the Smithsonian Institution and the Huntington Galleries.

Dr. Ann Gilbert McDonald. In addition to the important information in her book *The Evolution of the Night Lamp*, Ann has undertaken many hours of research for me at the Library of Congress in Washington.

Nancy O. Merrill. Curator of Glass at the Chrysler Museum and formerly curator of the Sandwich Glass Museum, Nancy has regularly added to my knowledge of kerosene lamps.

Dr. John W. Courter, the author of *Aladdin – The Magic Name in Lamps* is recognized as the leading authority on Aladdin lamps. Bill started the chain of events that led to my writing and producing three books between Oil Lamps I and Oil Lamps II.

I was privileged to meet two authors whose works are among those I consulted most frequently. In Maine I visited Lowell Innes, author of *Pittsburgh Glass 1797-1891* and in Florida I spent many hours with Dr. Arthur Peterson, author of *Glass Patterns and Patents*, as well as other books relating to glass and trade-marks.

Correspondence with Peter Cuffley, author of *Oil and Kerosene Lamps in Australia* has revealed that we share another common interest; he is currently preparing a book on gardens.

Three collectors who have generously shared documentation of kerosene lighting are: Kerry T. Bachler, Charles McGurk, Immediate Past President of the Rushlight Club and R.A. Harvey Snyder, President of The Historical Lighting Society of Canada.

There were others, as well, who shared their collections and primary source material, some of which is included in this book and the balance I hope to use in future publications. Each contribution has been unique and very significant. They are:

Gerry and Joanne Bloxom, Don and Joyce Blyth, Mary Boles, Doug and Joan Bone, Mr. & Mrs. Lawrence Bonner, Joyce Burne, Hugh Buzzard, James Bisback, John and Dorothy Dobson, Bret Farnum, Fernand (Fat) Fleurant, Maribeth Gellatly, Jonny Kalish, Cam Kenny,

Jack Kiener, Dr. Harvey Linzon, Mabel Lomas, Colin McLeod, F. Hollister McQuin, Tom and Beverly Mileham, Toni and Sharon Millengen, Jim Miller, Cornelia Mollard, Tom Neale, Ron and Anne Pavlovich, Cliff Peterson, Tom and Helen Porter, Olin and Barbara Rowoth, Arthur Sanders, Glen Schlotfeldt, Herb and Eileen White.

During the past seven years a surprising number of nineteenth and early twentieth-century catalogues, price lists, invoices, advertisements, trade publications, and other primary source material, as well as photographs of lamps, have come to light. While some of this belongs to the private collectors mentioned above, public institutions and company archives have ever-expanding collections of this type of important information, along with their examples of glass and lighting artifacts. The willingness to share it has been overwhelming. Credit for material from public institutions and from companies, is noted with the illustrations used. These sources are acknowledged here along with the names of those who were so generous with their time and gracious with their assistance.

The Chrysler Museum, Norfolk, VA. Nancy O. Merill, Curator of Glass.

Coalport China Works Museum, Telford (Ironbridge Gorge) Shropshire, England. Marc Pemberton.

The Corning Museum of Glass, Corning, N.Y. Jane S. Spillman, Curator of American Glass. Priscilla Price, Registrar. Norma Jenkins, Librarian. Virginia Wright, Associate Librarian.

The Dudley Metropolitan Borough Art Gallery, Dudley, West Midlands, England. Charles R. Hajdamach, Keeper, Glass and Fine Arts.

The Henry Ford Museum, Dearborn, MI. Kenneth M. Wilson, Director of Collections and Preservation. Bob Bowditch and Catharine Twork.

The Henry Francis du Pont Winterthur Museum. Winterthur, DE. Dr. Frank H. Sommer, Chief Librarian. Richard McKinstry, Associate Librarian. Kathryn McKenney, Librarian, Photography and Slide collection.

The Huntington Galleries, Huntington, WV. Roberta Emerson, Director. G. Eason Eige, Chief Curator. Dan Silosky, Registrar.

The Jones Gallery of Glass & Ceramics, Sebago, ME. Dorothy-Lee Jones.

Lightner Museum, St. Augustine, FL. Robert Harper, Director. Irene Lewis Miller, Registrar.

The Margaret Woodbury Strong Museum, Rochester, NY. Susan R. Williams, Associate Curator of Decorative Arts.

The National Archives, Polar and Scientific Branch, Washington, DC. Lee Johnson.

The National Museum of American History, Smithsonian Institution, Washington, DC. Anne M. Serio, Museum Specialist, Division of Domestic Life. Sheila Alexander, Museum Specialist Division of Ceramics and Glass.

Oglebay Institute Mansion Museum, Wheeling, WV. T. Patrick Brennan, Director.

Old Sturbridge Village, Sturbridge, MA. Theresa Rini Percy, Librarian.

The Royal Ontario Museum, Toronto, ON. Janet Holmes, Curatorial Assistant, Canadiana Department. Peter Kaellgren, Curatorial Fellow, European Department.

To those who have worked so enthusiastically in the mechanical preparation of this book, the artists, typesetters, proofreaders, technicians, color and printing experts, I extend my sincere thanks.

Nora Baranyai, Jack Cooper, Ana Lagowski, Keith Leonard, Fred Littlechild, Nina Marcotte, Joe Matiasek, Brenda Mitchell, Earl Patte, Nicole Sirois, Naznin Sunderji.

Hundreds of photographs were taken on location in situations that were often less than ideal and sometimes just barely adequate. Many of these, originally intended for reference only, have been included where the importance of the example and interest of the reader was deemed sufficient to warrant it. I am grateful to those who permitted me to take photographs, gave advice and information, wrote letters and sent photographs and assisted in a variety of other ways. These include:

Allen's Antiques, Arnholm Antiques, Richard and Dorothy Axtel, Albert Barnett, Molly Batram, The Bruce Becons, Dottie and Dan Besant, Joan Bleier, Rae Bloch, Peter and Marian Blundell, Paul Bosy, Richard Bourne, George Bowing, Alan and Kathy Bright, Alan Brook, Menzo and Anne Brown, Edna Brown, Paul C. Byington, Robert Calvin, Don and Jane Caskinette, Ruth Cathcart, Chez-nous Antiques, Earl Clark, Bernice Cohen, Bill Cole, Helen Cook, Lawrence and Mabel Cooke, Russell K. Cooper, Jowe and Pauline Creighton, Mr. & Mrs. Stanley Cross, Dan Cutini, David B. Dalzell, Jr., George and Mavinia Darrow, John A. Davis, Davison's Antiques, Ron Dawkins, Wendy Daxon, Larry De Can, De Groot's Antiques, George Downing, Linda Du Charme, Woody and Joyce Dyer, Sally and Elizabeth Earle, Tom Early, Ray and Marylin Ebbert, John and Christine Eecloo, Pat and Earl Eggleston, Richard Else, Milt Everhart, R. Farnan, Carl Fauster, Jim and Osna Fenner, Dr. Regis and Mary Ferson, Fire House Antiques, Ronald L. French, Rick and JoAnne Fuerst, Louise and Betty Gatter, Dorothy Gooch, Don Grant, Dorothy Haines, Harry W. Holmes, Bill and Wendy Hamilton, Clifford D. Hanson, Lawrence and Jean Hartnell, William Hawkes, W.T. Hentbore, Paul Hollister, David Hollowbush, George and Louise Horstick, Doreen Howard, Gilbert Hutchinson, Ruth Ingram, Ruth Irvine, Jamison's Antiques, Linda and Ed Julikowski, George and June Kelm, Dorothy Knapp, June C. Kobus, Lamplighter Shop, Herb and Gale Leflet, Dr. & Mrs. Robert Le Verre, Thomas C. Lindsey, Joseph Link, Eric and Val Lister, Richard Lobb, Lock, Stock and Barrel, Bryon Martin, Tom and Elizabeth Martin, C.J. Maurer, John McBain, C.F. McDougall, Pat McMahon, Glenn and Maureen McKellar, Karl Means, George E. Michael, William Frost Mobley, Bob and Chris Monts, David and Sandy Moore, Leigh Moore, Jack Morris Gallery, David Moskal, Herb Nelson, John Nichols, Nyce's Antiques, Grant Oakes, Sheldon Parks, Joyce Pickering, Gina Plastino, Mary L. Purdy, Carl C. Pyle, Mary Quasey, Dr. & Mrs. Leonard S. Rackow, Bertrand Rancourt, Marvin H. Ray, Robert R. Reed, The Reid Girls at Brimfield, Howard and Doris Reiss, Virginia Renschen, Robert M. Reynolds, Robert L. Rice, D & J Ritchie Auctioneers, Harry J. Robinson, Blanche Rogers, James and Margaret Ross, Arthur A. Ronat, Irving and Dot Sadowsky, Art and Kim Solomon, Duane and Nancy Sand, Sawdey's Antiques, John and Patricia Schadt, Richard and Magaret Shafer, Milton Shedivy, Sydney Schoom, Anne Serra, Kay Shelley, Steve Sherlock, Jon Silver, Diane Simard, Bea Simmons, David G. Smith, Edna Smith, Fred Smith, Linda Smith, Doris Bridges Soldner, Henry Stevenson, Phyllis Stewart, George and Helen Storey, Arthur L. Strom, Cleo B. Tidball, John and E.P. Tyler, Joe Valerio, Waddingtons Auctioneers, Dick and Barbara Willhoff, Carolyn B. Wilson, La Veta Woody, Carrie B. Yeary, Paul Zammit.

A special thanks to my good friend Hyla Fox. In addition to her role as columnist for the *Toronto Daily Star* and the *Maine Antique Digest,* she has completed a most informative and useful book for collectors, *Antiques: An Illustrated Guide for the Canadian Collector.* It is scheduled to be off the press at approximately the same time as this book. Constant communication has enabled us to commiserate with and cajole each other throughout the isolation that is an inevitable part of writing.

The most important contributor to the production of this book is my husband Carl. His support, encouragement and enjoyment of the entire venture, coupled with his discerning eye and expertise in every area of publishing, made it all happen. Our horizons and our circle of friends continue to expand with each book.
These are the true rewards!

Contents

The Glass Kerosene Lamp Nomenclature

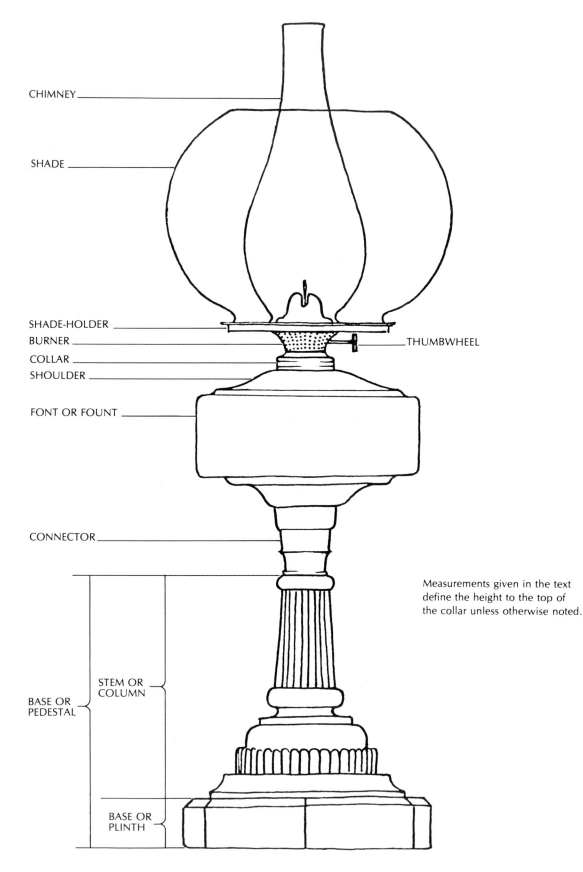

CHIMNEY

SHADE

SHADE-HOLDER

BURNER

THUMBWHEEL

COLLAR

SHOULDER

FONT OR FOUNT

CONNECTOR

Measurements given in the text define the height to the top of the collar unless otherwise noted.

STEM OR COLUMN

BASE OR PEDESTAL

BASE OR PLINTH

Glass and Glassmaking

Glass was the most common material used for kerosene lamps. As a container for oil, glass had the advantage of being impervious, leakproof, and inexpensive; and the disadvantage of being breakable. Both this fragility and the vicissitudes of Victorian fashion resulted in the attrition and obsolescence of lamps and chimneys. This, coupled with a huge increase in domestic and foreign markets, added a tremendous blown-glass production to that of the popular pressed-glass tableware.

It was pure coincidence that the kerosene era, beginning in the late 1850's, paralleled both the pressed-glass tableware period and several decades of innovative glassmaking in the United States. That the study of kerosene lamps relies to a great extent upon the published research of glass scholars is obvious; but the fact that the study of kerosene lamps may contribute to the body of knowledge of glass of this period is scarcely recognized. Herein lies the challenge to explore this potential. An understanding of the basic methods of manufacture, and knowledge of the terminology, will expand the appreciation of both glass and lamps.

Most North American glass lamps were made in two geographical areas. Factories in the East, located mainly in Massachusetts, are generally referred to as the New England companies. The largest production was in the Ohio river valley and surrounding areas that included parts of Pennsylvania, Ohio and West Virginia. This was known as the Midwest, and it is still the name given to the region by glass scholars.

Passages from an 1863 issue of *The Scientific American* and the writings of glassmaker Harry Bastow in 1908 and 1920,[1] are included wherever direct quotation is deemed to be the most informative and accurate presentation of certain aspects of glassmaking during the 1860 to 1920 period.

Glass Composition

Glass is the product of fusion (by melting), of silica with other ingredients, that affect its manufacture and appearance. *Metal* is a term used by the trade to describe glass either in its molten or finished state.

Glass formulas or recipes include the following ingredients:

SILICA usually in the form of *sand*.

FLUXES that allow the ingredients to melt and combine at a lower temperature. These include *alkalies* such as *soda* or *potash*, and broken glass referred to as *cullet*.

A STABILIZER such as *lime* or *lead*.

COLORANTS usually in the form of mineral salts or metallic oxides. Manganese was used as both a colorant, and as a decolorizer to counteract the common green color imparted by iron impurities in the raw materials.

FLINT GLASS HOUSE

View of the Inside of the Flint Glass Furnace

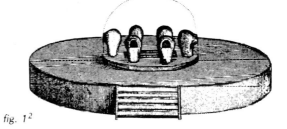

fig. 1[2]

The most brilliant lamps and tableware were made of lead glass, also referred to as crystal or flint glass (generic if not accurate terms that have evolved), or of soda-lime glass. In 1864 a soda-lime formula using bicarbonate of soda was developed by William Leighton at Hobbs Brockunier & Company in Wheeling, WV. Reheated or fire-polished fonts made with this formula may be difficult to distinguish from those made with lead glass. Experiments using ultraviolet light to detect lead content show that lead glass was used for some lamps throughout the nineteenth century kerosene period. Less refined bottle glass was rarely used for lamps.

Glass Production

Glass factories had *furnaces* that contained *pots* made of clay in which raw ingredients known as the *batch* were melted. The glass was shaped while in its molten and plastic state. Access to the glass, which was heated to over 2000°F, was through a *work hole*. Smaller furnaces, with one or more openings called *glory-holes*, were used to reheat articles for further shaping or for *fire polishing* to remove mold marks. The intense heat became unbearable in the hot weather, and for this reason it was usual for factories to shut down during the summer months.

In the nineteenth century a team comprised of about five men called a *shop* worked together to produce glass objects. A *move* was the term used to describe the number of pieces a shop was expected to make during a half-day period (four to five hours), and a *turn* was the half-day period itself. The *gaffer*, or head of the group, was the most skilled and responsible for the quality of the articles produced. On kerosene hand lamps his "final touch" fashioned the *stuck* or *applied* handle.

To work the glass a few basic tools were used. These I will describe in an outline of the method used to make a blown font or container known as a hollow vessel.

The *blowpipe*, an iron pipe about four to six feet long and slightly flared at the end, was turned rapidly by the *gatherer* in the pot of viscid, molten glass to pick up a *gather*. It was then rolled on a metal or marble slab called a *marver*, or rotated on or within a concave wooden *block*, kept wet to prevent sticking or charring. These operations formed a thin skin on the glass and lessened the danger of distortion or a blowout.

After this *marvering* or *blocking*, the *gather* was reheated and air blown into the *blowpipe* to expand the glass into a bubble or *parison*. It was then shaped either in a *mold* (or *matrix*), or shaped with a spring tool called a *pucella* or *jack*. Shaping could be done while the glass was on the blowpipe or after it was transferred to an iron rod called a *pontil rod* or *punty*. Modifications and improvisations added a variety of other tools to facilitate certain operations.

Annealing was the next step undertaken to prevent the glass from cooling with stresses that could cause it later to crack or even explode. The glass was either cooled or reheated; whichever was required to bring it all to a uniform temperature of about 1000°F. Then it was slowly conveyed for several hours through an annealing oven or *lehr*, until it was reduced to room temperature.

Not all methods of glass manufacture are completely understood or possible to ascertain, nor is there complete agreement on terminology past or present. Most of the confusion regarding blown glass terminology i.e.: Blown Three Mold, Insufflated etc., involves glass made before 1850 and is not a concern in the study of kerosene lamps. Nineteenth century glass kerosene lamps are generally identified by the basic techniques used. These are: *free-blown*, *mold-blown* or *pressed*.

FREE-BLOWN. This is a widely accepted term used to describe objects made without the use of a mold. The final shape is achieved by a combination of manual dexterity and the glassmaker's tools.

Off-hand is another term for the free-blown technique, particularly used to describe the non-commercial items made by the glassmakers during their lunch time or after hours. In a twentieth century account, it has also been applied to human as opposed to machine-blown glass.

MOLD-BLOWN. Most kerosene fonts were blown into a full-size mold having two or more parts. *Mold-blown*, the most common term used to describe this technique, is the one used by Lowell Innes and Jane Spillman, and the one I will use. Another term, *blown-molded* used by Helen McKearin and Kenneth M. Wilson[1] is closer to the term *blow-molded* used today by manufacturers of plastic bottles.

Molds were most commonly made of a superior quality expensive iron; but brass, bronze and wooden molds were also used. For a smoother surface they were often coated inside with a paste made of carbon and oil. Some glass companies designed and made their own molds, while others purchased them from mold makers who could supply stock or custom designs. Custom-made molds, known as private molds, were made for specific companies who contracted with a glass factory to supply quantities of the molded glass objects. Wholesalers, retailers or other glass companies could have availed themselves of this service.

Mold-blown fonts will usually have two or more mold seams radiating from the neck or collar opening, and sometimes horizontal mold seams. These mold seams may be cleverly disguised in a shape or pattern. Plain mold-blown fonts were often made in shapes that today closely resemble common free-blown shapes. If rotated in the mold before removal, or fire polished, (possibly in preparation for surface decoration), it may require careful scrutiny to determine how they were made. Patterned fonts will have an exterior that conforms to the interior of the mold. The interior of the font will correspond with the exterior, and the extent to which this occurs is dependent upon the thickness of the glass.

The number of parts that comprise a mold may have some significance for research purposes, but little or none for the aesthetic or monetary value of the lamp.

PRESSED GLASS. Molds for pressed glass articles were designed to permit a plunger (usually with a corresponding shape) to be inserted and withdrawn. Molten glass, cut off a gather, was dropped into the mold. The plunger then forced it to assume the mold shape and pattern. Most glass lamp bases were pressed.

Pressed glass fonts required manipulation when released from the mold, to draw in the open portion. This generally formed the collar but in some instances the bottom of the mold formed the collar, and the drawn-in part had a peg fused to it.

As with the mold-blown technique, the font could be plain or patterned. Sometimes a patterned plunger was used in combination with a plain mold with the result that the pattern was inside or "under glass." *Plunger-patterned* would describe these fonts more accurately, and would distinguish this type from techniques which allowed a pattern to be trapped inside or "within the walls."[1] Lamps made by this method are very attractive when empty or filled with water, but when kerosene is used their appearance suffers. The refractive quality of kerosene virtually obliterates the pattern, however this didn't seem to deter substantial production judging by the numbers extant.

Many Midwest glass companies made fonts by a method called *optic-molded*. Blown fonts produced by this technique have a soft undulating pattern seen through a smooth exterior. In order to achieve this two molds were used; *(figs. 3, 4 & 5)* a patterned one and a larger plain one. A gather of glass was first blown into the smaller patterned mold to produce a font with relatively large and distinct protrusions. Raised circles or ribs were most common. Still attached to the blowpipe the font was removed from the patterned mold and placed inside the smooth larger mold. When the glass blower further expanded the font against the smooth interior of the mold, it forced the thick projections to the inside of the font for the desired effect. The softness of the pattern distinguishes optic-molded fonts from the faceted or shaped designs made by pressing.

Common Imperfections

The quality of a piece of glass reflects the skills and artistry of the glassworker and reveals the talents of the designers and moldmakers.

Tools and techniques sometimes left telltale imperfections that are often admired today as indications of handmade quality. Their causes and recognizable effects are as follows:

Worn or poorly matched mold parts left fins or beads of glass along the mold seams.

Breaking the base off the pontil rod (punty) resulted in a rough scar that was sometimes ground off leaving a circular depression.

A mold that had not been properly heated before use resulted in a temperature differential that prevented uniform contact. This created the whittled or dimpled appearance referred to by collectors as chill marks, or by the trade as *cold mold*.

Threads of glass that formed when a gather was withdrawn from the pot, were sometimes picked up on a subsequent gather; leaving lines called *striae* or *cords*[2] on the surface of the glass. *(fig. 2)*

Tiny bubbles, called *seeds,* occurred both in lamps and chimneys.

Glass is a very corrosive material that will eat away the pot or container. Particles of the pot sometimes cause streaks or specks within the glass. These and other impurities or bits of unmelted batch are called *stones*. They are particularly noticeable on white pressed bases.

The surface of glass in a pot will have a tendency to devitrify. This results in a scum that has the appearance of flecks or impurities within the finished piece. Today the trade describes examples with this problem as "scummy glass."

Cold shears, used to cut off glass for pressed glass molding, could leave a line or fold, sometimes called a *straw mark*, or more correctly, a *shear mark*.

If the glass did not properly fill the mold in either a blowing or pressing operation, the resultant indentation is called a *mold underfill*.

Chimney Production

Lamp chimneys were either pressed, mold-blown or free-blown. The following account from *The Scientific American* provides a detailed description, (with possibly some inaccuracies in reporting) of how free-blown chimneys were made in 1863:[3]

"The chimneys of lamps are formed by blowing. A boy takes a straight iron tube, about five feet in length, dips one of its ends into the pot containing molten glass, gives it a few turns, and winds a sufficient quantity upon it to make a chimney. It is then carried to a smooth iron table on which the glass is gently rolled to smooth it; then the blower puffs a blast down the tube which expands the glass bulb like a bubble of soap; he then gives his tube a few swings like a pendulum, when the plastic glass at its lower ends elongates into a tube. In order to form the swollen part on its lower end, the operator rests it upon the floor and gives a slight puff down his tube, when it bulges out in the well-known form of a glass chimney—a globe with a long neck. The lower end is now broken off and opened with a tool, and the neck is also separated from the blowing rod. The chimney has now to undergo two other operations, another furnace with round holes in it being used for this purpose. A second operative places the chimney upon an iron rod and thrusts its lower end into the mouth of a furnace until it becomes quite plastic with the heat. He now withdraws it, lays his rod horizontally upon an iron bench and rolls it with his left hand, while with his right he spins out the mouth of the chimney, [sic] and turns the flange upon it with a tool which also gages the size. A boy now presses a small red-hot iron disk upon the end of a rod against the under flange of the chimney, and it sticks fast to it, when the chief operator thrusts its neck into an open hole in the same furnace, gives it a few turns, takes it out, rolls it with his left hand upon the table, and with his right guiding a tool, he smooths the neck of the chimney; then he places it upon a bench and disengages it finished from his rod in a dexterous manner. In this way glass lamp chimneys are blown and finished without being placed in an annealing furnace. A set of operatives consisting of two men and five boys make seventy-five dozen of chimneys per day."

fig. 2 Chimney with striae or cords

Color and Decoration

Although colorless glass, usually referred to as clear, was the most common material, opaque, transluscent and transparent colors, and complex mixtures and methods were also used. In addition, the various types of surface decoration found on tableware and decorative pieces, was used on kerosene lamps.

Opalescent glass that has red to fiery orange and yellow highlights when back lit, was used for lamps and shades. Glass made with a special heat sensitive formula, was reheated to create the desirable accented white opalescent areas. White, colored, transluscent and nearly opaque opalescent lamps were made primarily in the 1850's and 1860's.

In the 1880's, 1890's and early in this century, lamps, shades, pitchers, tumblers and tableware were made with white opalescent accents and patterns; particularly spots and stripes. To achieve these opalescent accents, the glass was blown into a mold with a deeply cut intaglio design (fig. 3) to produce a font with a pronounced raised pattern. After it was removed it was subjected to a blast of cold air and then quickly reheated at the glory hole. (fig. 4) The raised parts that were closest to the fire assumed the opalescent accents. For optic-molded spots the glass was further expanded in a smooth mold. (fig. 5) Sometimes two layers of glass were used, one colored and the other a colorless one having the heat sensitive formula.

Opalescent patterned fonts were almost always optic-molded. If there were opalescent spots, the interior of the first mold would have had dome-shaped indentations. If the spots were transparent colorless or colored glass, surrounded by an opalescent white area, the first mold would have had raised domes on the inside. Opalescent spots have also been described as dots and polka dots, and transparent spots as windows. Opalescent stripes and patterns were of course achieved in the same manner.

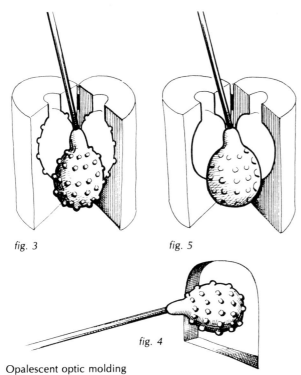

fig. 3   fig. 5

fig. 4

Opalescent optic molding

Early Art Glass lamps were made in the 1850's and 1860's. Types included silvered glass, overshot (craquelle) with crushed glass embedded in the surface and those made with threads of glass in contrasting colors that were spiralled, crossed (lattice or latticinio) or looped. During the Art Glass period that began about 1880 the well-known types of Art Glass such as Agata, Burmese, Cameo, Crown Milano, Peach Blow, Pearl Satinware and Royal Flemish were used primarily for vase, student and hanging lamps. Marble and spatter glass was also used

throughout the nineteenth century kerosene era for stand lamps, and for very special shades. Although the range of glass types is not quite as broad as that used for decorative pieces or accessories, kerosene lamps were certainly decorative as well as necessary functional articles.

Surface decoration is referred to as extrinsic decoration by Helen McKearin to distinguish it as an art form separate from that of the glassmaker. To make it permanent, some surface decoration such as painting, enamelling, staining and gilding was subjected to a reheating and cooling process akin to annealing. Less permanent were the typically late Victorian paper transfers, pastiche and marbleized effects obtained by dipping the lamp into oil colors floated on water. These could have been created at the factory or at home.

Three techniques used to produce a matt finish on glass were grinding, sandblasting and the very common acid etching. Frosted Glass is a safe and accurate way to describe glass that has a matt finish. Satin or camphor glass are other names that also describe the appearance, rather than the process used to achieve the effect. Frosted glass was produced by the following methods:

Sandblasting: Grains of sand forced by air pressure through a nozzle, bombarded the surface of the glass giving it a rough texture. This process appears to have been used to decorate fonts and shades from about 1875 on.

Acid etching: The finest texture was achieved by acid etching, and hydrofluoric acid was most commonly used. Different acids were said to have been employed to produce different textures, but the extent to which this was done and the recognizable effects are not possible to determine. Acids were also used to give a polished finish to cut glass.

The glass was either immersed in the acid or exposed to its fumes. A resist such as wax applied to selected surfaces before etching, allowed these areas to remain unaffected.

Cameo glass was deeply etched (to the base color) in preparation for carving the outer layer or layers. A cameo effect was often produced on lamp shades by deeply etching the area surrounding a more coarsely textured matt surface, created first by grinding.

Acid etching was commonly combined with ruby staining and gilding on fonts. These lamps circa 1870 appear to be among the first examples of acid etched lamps.

Grinding: This method was used extensively on shades and fonts. It was described in 1863 in *The Scientific American:*[1]

"Globes for lamps are ground dull on the surface (to tone the light) by being placed in a lathe, and made to revolve while a pad containing sand and water is held against them."

Another source from the 1870's described a brush rather than a pad used with sand.[2] The texture created by grinding on a lathe may be coarse or very fine. The frosted bands on shades and the frosted areas surrounding pressed designs on fonts, were mostly produced on a lathe. Such shades and fonts were advertised and referred to by the trade as *roughed.*

Also described in *The Scientific American* article was a method used to grind the interior of shades:

> "Some globes are also rendered dull in their interior. This is effected by placing a small quantity of sand and fine gravel with some water in each, then placing several in a long narrow box in which they are snugly secured among hay, and the box is then made to revolve. The sand and gravel seek the center of gravity, while the globes in revolving rub against the sand and gravel."

Early kerosene and pre-kerosene shades of various shapes and sizes are found with coarsely ground interiors. Their greyish color and shiny surface appear rather like a light bulb or television tube.

Cut and engraved glass was also produced by grinding. Again, *The Scientific American* description outlines the process, and includes information that should be of interest to those who study all glass of this period:

> "We will now describe the operations of cutting-flint glass. The cutting of glass is conducted in the second and third stories of the manufactory. Here let us premise that glass-cutting is not executed with diamond or steel cutting tools, as many persons suppose. Glass-cutting is a system of grinding with small revolving stones. The main cutting room has a row of wheels on each side, numbering altogether over fifty. These are driven by belting, just like grindstones. As much light is necessary to perform the operations, each wheel is placed before a window, and above it, is an inverted conical trough containing water, a stream of which is made to trickle upon the stone. The stones are small and narrow; and some are plane in the face, while others are formed with a beveled circular edge running round the middle. We saw bottles, decanters, stoppers and various other articles undergoing the cutting operations. Diamond-checkered bottles, flowered globes, prismatic stoppers and all the various patterns are cut by these fine revolving stones. A bottle or other article is held by the glass-cutter against his revolving stone, and the pattern is ground upon it according to the skill of the operative. The face of the wheels or stones are different in shape for the grinding of different patterns. The stones for fine grinding are obtained from Craigleith quarry in Scotland, the coarse ones from Newcastle, England. The cutting of glass by grinding renders the surface dull; it is afterwards polished on a buffing wheel with a powder composed of the oxides of tin and lead. Some articles, however, are cut with dull flowers and figures upon polished surfaces. The holes in the necks of crystal bottles are ground accurately by being centered in a revolving chuck, and stoppers are ground in the same lathe to fit air-tight.
> The very finest cutting on glass, however, is here executed with a small revolving copper disk in a lathe, the grinding agent being oil and emery. Beautiful patterns, figures, names, &c., are thus executed on polished crystal articles. Great skill and taste are demanded in such operations. The cutting resembles the lines executed on steel plates with a graver. We examined one small drinking-cup which was a splendid specimen of glass-cutting. Its sides were laid out in panels; in one was the figure of a deer; in another a glass-house, and in another a cathedral. A cast of all new patterns is taken in plaster, so as to reproduce the article should it ever be called for. The first-class articles manufactured in this establishment are transluscent as rock crystal itself. The cost of each chiefly depends upon the labour bestowed upon it in the cutting operation."

All of these surface decorations could have been produced at the glass factory, or by another company that finished undecorated pieces or blanks.

Glass Types & Terminology

Transparent Glass: Allows you to see through it. It may be colorless or colored and of course the amount of colorants will affect the degree of transparency.

Transluscent Glass: Diffuses light and softens the definition of images behind it to the extent that they may become mere shadowy areas.

Opaque: White or colored glass which appears to be opaque in average light situations approximating intended use. Intense natural or artificial light may reveal other characteristics. Transparent and transluscent lamps emphasize their vitreous (glass-like) nature, while opaque lamps often resemble china or porcelain.

Most nineteenth and twentieth century trade publications and retail advertising referred to opaque white glass as opal (pronounced as o-pal'). Milk glass, the most common term heard today was known but little used in the nineteenth century. Usage has determined that opal and milk glass are appropriate terms for opaque white and sometimes colored glass, but the term opaque is more accurate by definition and less confusing to the layman.

A simple guide to opacity would be to consider the piece opaque if you cannot see your finger behind it under average light (not back lit) conditions.

Opalescent: Mentioned earlier, this glass refracts light with rainbow colors, particularly orange and yellow. It may be transluscent, transparent or opaque (as described above) and may require strong natural or artificial light to see the opalescence. White pieces often have a decidedly bluish cast, particularly in the thinner areas and some examples look almost like alabaster described below.

Alabaster: The terms opaline, clambroth or clam-water are commonly, but perhaps not too comfortably, used to describe the glass that was made and sold as alabaster. In OL I the glass I referred to as opaline is essentially the same as that called opaline by other writers, but evidence now strongly suggests these lamps are more correctly identified as alabaster. The number of times the name alabaster has occurred in the description of glass and lamps during the kerosene period, necessitates its introduction. Documentary evidence is noted in the Appendix.

Alabaster glass is non-opalescent and can range from opaque to nearly transparent.

If it is opaque, its granular quality makes it distinguishable from opal or milk glass. The surface varies from coarse, (sometimes due to deterioration), to smooth — almost greasy. It can be faintly to obviously granular and it might have white flecks. The general appearance ranges from very fine to very poor.

Not every glass or lamp company advertised alabaster glass even though they are known to have made it. Both Atterbury & Co. and Ripley & Company made examples of their patented lamps in alabaster glass.

Whenever glass cannot be examined closely, or if its category appears to be borderline, it is more accurate to describe its apparent characteristics.

Cased and Cut

Kerosene lamps with two or more contrasting layers of glass were made mainly during two periods. The first period was from the late 1850's to the late 1870's, and the second period was from about 1880 to 1910. In 1859 the S. E. Southlands catalogue described them as plated, and those of the second period were advertised as cased. During the first period it was the custom to cut away the outside layer or layers to reveal the base color. The concave cut areas became wide-angle lenses. They focus on a large part of the opposite interior, and a colorless glass base layer most effectively illustrates this often dazzling manifestation. The quality of this special glass, and the workmanship varied greatly. Today, for these early lamps, neither the term plated nor the term cased is used to any extent, but rather the term overlay or occasionally Bohemian. Thus we have cased, plated, overlay and Bohemian commonly used to describe lamps made with two or more layers of glass. Cased glass blanks were used for the exquisite English carved cameo glass lamps. In America the most complex and skilfully made lamps were produced from 1850 on. Most of these involved cutting, engraving and decorating layered glass. In order to adopt terminology for the many examples illustrated in this book, an examination of techniques and terms is in order.

During the first half of the nineteenth century, Bohemia, then a part of Austria and now part of Czechoslovakia, established a world-wide reputation for making the finest layered, colored, cut and decorated glass. "Bohemian glass" has been a generic term for this glass for over one hundred and thirty years. The superiority of the skill and technology this glass exhibited was unquestioned; however, the artistic quality has always received mixed reviews. Clumsy and garish imitations have given rise to the pejorative use of "Bohemian" as a generic term.

Cased and plated are terms that pre-date 1860, while overlay seems to be a twentieth century description. Cased is the one term that was used before and throughout the kerosene period by the trade and in advertising. It is the one that I will use to describe layered glass.

Three methods used to produce layered glass have been described in nineteenth and twentieth century literature. The first involved blowing separate cup shapes or shells, placing one within the other, and shaping the article after these were fused to the final parison. Several thin layers could be built up with this process, used for the cased and cut lamps so popular during the 1860's. One of the chief difficulties inherent in blowing into the shell or casing, was the possibility of entrapment of air between the layers, causing a blister or bubble.

The second method commonly involved the use of "rolls" of colored glass that were made up ahead of time. These rolls or "balls" as they were described in an old handwritten glassmaker's formula notebook,[1] were made in different colors and kept on hand to be used as required. According to Frank M. Fenton[2] their ruby cased glass is made from rolls about 12" long and 2-1/2" in diameter using a formula that contains coin gold. When the batch is first melted it is almost colorless. The rolls are allowed to cool to room temperature and then slowly reheated until the red or ruby color develops.

It is interesting that in 1908 Bastow[3] does not refer to the first method of casing used for cased and cut lamps. He states that: "In the case of such articles as vases, fruit bowls, etc., in cased effects, the inside or cased color is usually worked from the "roll." He then outlines the procedure: "These rolls are carefully re-heated, and a small piece cut off the end of the roll and placed on the red-hot end of the blowpipe, and then worked into an incipient bubble. This is then dipped into the pot containing the glass to be used for the outside color, and the whole mass then blown into the shape required, the casing color, of course, expanding with the remainder of the glass, and forming a complete lining." He describes the effective use of this method with deep colors over white; however, for lamps, the most common use was for colorless glass over a base color. This method, which evolved as an economical use of colored glass, imparts a brilliance and lucidity to the finished article. Because the thickness of subsequent layers is more difficult to control, it is not considered to have been used for glass having more than two layers.

The third method, today called the "German Method" by the trade, was also often used to economize the more expensive colored glass. It involved a second dipping of glass over the initial one after it had been blocked and shaped. This is probably the method referred to by Bastow: "In such articles as white-lined shades, globes etc., in green and a number of other outside colors, the casing white is generally gathered direct from the pot, instead of being worked from rolls."

The German Method, described in current union agreements, refers to the procedure and can apply to either two colors or to a second layer from the same pot.[4] For successful fusion, cased glass required each of the layers to have the same coefficient of expansion. It is often difficult and sometimes impossible to determine the method that was used to make cased glass.

Hall, hanging and table lamps of the later period were made with cased glass that was rarely cut, but was sometimes acid etched to create a satin effect. A colorless outer layer particularly enhanced pointed hobnail shades, giving the clear tips an added sparkle.

Flashed glass is a term that has been used to describe cased glass or stained glass. Bastow notes that flashing differs from the casing method he described using rolls: "Only in that the incipient bubble of the casing color is burst open at the end, and this hole expands when the whole bulb expands, so that the casing color shows only toward the outer margin of the article". Confusion can be avoided if the correct description is used. During my recent glassmaking experience, "flashing" the glass meant a fast reheating in the glory hole, that was usually intended to maintain heat throughout the piece of glass and at the end of the blowpipe. This minimized stresses developing as the article was being shaped.

The dictionary defines casing as an outer layer or enclosure, however, the glassmaker's notes mentioned earlier, refer to "casing inside and out". In another instance, in a letter written by Frederick S. Shirley, agent for the Mt. Washington Glass Works, on paper dated ". . . 1895," he states that the formulas described: "stand both for inside and outside casing."[1]

Although glass researcher Paul Hollister has documented U.S. manufacture of cased and cut glass as early as 1847, and the solar lamp, (fig. 6), is dated 1843-1849, cased and cut lamps are seldom considered to have been made in North America before the late 1850's.[2]

Solar lamps, popular in the 1850's, were designed to burn whale oil or lard. They often had cased and cut stems, but the fonts, containing a central tube, were made of metal, usually brass. Factory modifications adapted the metal fonts for kerosene and these were combined with metal or cased and cut glass stems. The S. E. Southlands catalogue contains the earliest descriptions of cased and cut fonts.[3] It is to be hoped that future discoveries of primary source material will reveal examples of cased and cut lamps of the mid-fifties or earlier.

There is not only the possibility of attributing typically kerosene cased and cut lamps to an earlier period, but also the possibility of attributing the exclusive use of kerosene to some typically whale-oil and burning-fluid lamps. No. 1 brass collars, approximately 7/8" in diameter, have maintained a uniform size (with perhaps minute variations), from the first ones made in the 1830's, until today. The standard No. 2 kerosene lamp collar, with approximately 1-1/4" thread diameter, listed in the S. E. Southlands catalogue, may only have been a product of the kerosene period. While burning-fluid and whale-oil burners were commonly made to fit collars of a size larger than the No. 1, none has been found to fit a No. 2 collar. This suggests that lamps with No. 2 collars were made solely for kerosene. If so, many lamps considered to have been made for whale oil or burning fluid will have to be reclassified. It would have been a simple matter to finish pressed or blown lamps to take a No. 2 collar, and this might have been the practice when kerosene No. 2 size burners were introduced. These observations are speculative and are presented only as a suggestion for future research.

Advertisements and patents referred to both burning-fluid and fluid-burning lamps and burners. The former was a dangerous, potentially explosive mixture of alcohol and redistilled turpentine, and the latter simply referred to any liquid fuel, including kerosene.

Many patents were issued for the manufacture or design of glass. Some of these were specifically for lamps or shades, and some were applicable to a variety of objects including lamps.

The so-called one-piece pressed glass lamps, especially popular in the 1890's, were made throughout the kerosene period. The base, stem and font were pressed in one operation that left a wide opening at the top. This had to be reheated and drawn in to form a collar, or a separate shoulder was fused onto the top before annealing. Fully automated machines were introduced at the turn of the century.

While most color names have remained the same, yellow-green and sometimes light yellow are now referred to as vaseline. Ruby was the name given to almost any shade of red glass including that which we call cranberry today.

Black glass is often held to the light to see if a color is evident in the thinner portions. This is sometimes considered to be of special significance, however Bastow's description of black glass dispells any notion of this: "Black is commonly produced by using an excess of colorants which give effects that are largely complementary to each other, such as yellow, purple, blue, etc. This requires only that the colorants used should be compatible with the same batch conditions. The small amount of light that is transmitted through this glass is usually purple, blue, etc., according to which colorant is in greatest excess, but this is rarely of sufficient importance to require careful balancing for perfect neutralization, and, as a matter of fact, black glass is commonly used as a dumping ground for using up cullet of any and all colors."

Original pattern names will sometimes surface after twentieth century names have been established. Ideally, the original name should be adopted, but realistically, names are a means of communication and are difficult to change. Most patterns have been named by authors and there are many that are multi-named for various reasons. Very few patterns have their original names. I have endeavored to include all names and will indicate the original names that are known to me by the letters.[ON] It should be kept in mind that some manufacturers gave the same name to more than one pattern, or used different numbers for the same pattern in different catalogues. Also, some patterns made by more than one company have been given different names by the manufacturer.

fig. 6
Courtesy the Corning Museum of Glass

Attribution

Every owner of a lamp, whether a museum or private collector, wishes to know the origin of each piece they own. Authenticated pieces assume an importance, and often a monetary value that is sometimes far greater than that of a similar unidentified one. In view of the number of past attributions that have subsequently been found to be incorrect, it is wise to investigate the source and circumstances of the attribution.

Information derived from several sources should influence attributions. These sources include contemporary public and private records such as diaries, photographs and directories. Patent and trademark information usually provides a reliable basis for attribution, although errors or misinterpretation have occurred in this primary source material. Catalogues are also valuable contemporary sources. It should be kept in mind that the unbiased interpretation of all this material is vital to authentication and attribution.

Attribution may be made to an individual who was the designer or inventor, or to a company who made all or part of the lamp. Both nineteenth century and present-day companies have included in their catalogues, goods they assembled as well as ones made by other companies. While technically the attribution of such goods to these companies is valid, their role (if any) in the production of these examples should be stated. Advertised by, sold by, offered by, etc., would be more accurate descriptions if there is some doubt.

Glass, metal and other materials, are part of the bodies of most lamps. However, the predominant material in either proportion, or interest, may not be one that influenced the attribution you read or hear about. An example of this is the attribution of all-glass lamps (except for the collar) to Dietz & Company[1] (who did not make glass) and the attribution of an all-metal lamp to the Boston & Sandwich Glass Company[2] who made only glass.

This situation could be avoided if the credit were given to the person or company responsible for making the most significant part of the lamp. If two parts deserve recognition then a qualified attribution could be made to avoid confusion.

Not only does the same lamp turn up in more than one company's catalogue, it may have been popular enough to appear over a long period of time. My observations thus far indicate this occurs considerably less with lamps than with pressed glass tableware. The examination of one lamp extant, illustrated in both the Boston & Sandwich Glass Company catalogue, and the Dietz & Company catalogue has led to the discovery of a third company (Iden & Co.) associated with this lamp; plus the possibility of the involvement of a fourth company, the manufacturer of the metal parts. This is illustrated and described in the chapter on related lamps.

Oral history, the reminiscences of those whose recollections reveal important unrecorded information, can be very valuable; *provided the facts are accurate.*

The cullet used as a flux in glassmaking, has often been found or excavated at the former site of a glass company. These fragments of glass are sometimes called *shards* or *sherds* after the word potsherd, the piece of broken pottery used to cover the hole in the bottom of a flower pot. Some glass formulas show cullet comprised half or more of the ingredients by weight. If a company couldn't supply this from its routine breakage and rejects, it may have bought cullet from another source. This would have applied particularly to companies starting up initially, or after a fire. Considerable conjecture has been expressed regarding the subject of cullet, but little is really known about how or where it was sold, exchanged or acquired.

Fragments found at a glass factory site do not necessarily represent cullet produced at that factory. Great caution should be exercised in the interpretation of this material.

In the 1960's, researchers were beginning to change the tide of opinion that had considered the discovery of shards sufficient evidence upon which to base attribution. Today, such a find without any supportive contextual evidence would not be considered reliable proof by authorities associated with any of the U.S. museums that have significant glass collections.

In Canada, questionable and sometimes completely unfounded attributions have been made to Canadian glass companies. Attributions based on information obtained from museum excavations and private digs, have encouraged Canadian importation of large quantities of American glass. These pieces sold at much higher prices because they were labelled "Canadian."

Until we discover substantial supportive evidence to warrant attribution, the majority of today's "Burlington" lamps and glass patterns should only be regarded as North American. It is unfortunate that in the absence of an official report on the Burlington Glass Works archaeological excavations by the Royal Ontario Museum, misinformation is allowed to be perpetuated and promulgated. Researchers and collectors must accept the fact that some of the pieces of the puzzle have been lost forever, and that the ultimate goal is knowledge of exactly what is fact. From this base, a personal evaluation may be formulated, but fact and opinion should always be defined.

Accessory Parts Illustrated

The shades illustrated in this book are old and appropriate, if not original. All shade holders and burners in the Foreign Lamps section are probably original. Accessories in other sections were the most suitable ones available.

Opposite ▷

Eaton[ON] or Onion Lamps.
Exceptional design and glass quality combine to make these alabaster glass lamps c.1870, the most exquisite expression of the kerosene era, in the opinion of this writer. These lamps are described on page 44.

Related Lamps

Eaton ON

Related Lamps

Probably the most interesting method of research involves the comparison of actual examples, and the evaluation of the information discovered. Glass lamp parts that were pressed or mold-blown exhibit characteristics of the mold used, and those that can be proven to have been made in the same mold are the most significant. This also applies to cast metal parts.
Examination of similar lamps will place them in one of the following four categories:

1. Made from the same mold.

2. Made from an identical mold (possibly the same mold).

3. Made from a similar mold (possibly the same mold).

4. Made from a different mold.

The characteristics that determine the category of the relationship are:

1. MADE FROM THE SAME MOLD. The strongest evidence of this is the duplication of imperfections. The most common imperfections that I have seen duplicated are:

   (a) Identical extraneous protrusions or indentations caused by a mold or plunger with a defect or damage.

   (b) Overflow in a specific area along mold seams, due to an imperfect fit or damage.

   (c) Minute raised hairlines running across the two lowest horizontal planes of pressed bases like those shown on p. 20. They emanate and run outward from the junction of these planes and the vertical ribbing or square step. Three groups of bases, numbering from two to five, have been found, each group having lines of the same configuration. This would seem to me to preclude an overflow, and more logically would indicate fissures on iron molds, apparently caused by stress or developed through use.

   Mold imperfections may have developed at any time during the use of the mold; therefore a lack of imperfection does not preclude use of the same mold.

2. MADE FROM AN IDENTICAL MOLD. This is determined by pattern or proportion duplication. The same assymetrical variations of proportion in what was obviously intended to be a balanced design, or, the identical juxtaposition of pattern elements will determine if the pieces came from identical molds. Sometimes this can be easily determined and other times it may take a long time to examine every angle and aspect. Because comparing two examples with different types and/or colors of glass can be very difficult, daylight or strong artificial light is recommended.

3. MADE FROM A SIMILAR MOLD. If the design and execution of the parts appear to be symmetrical and flawless (and usually simple), and in the absence of precise scientific measurement facilities, it can only be stated that the examples appear to have been made in similar molds having the same degree of perfection and size.

4. MADE FROM A DIFFERENT MOLD. An obvious difference in design or proportion will determine this.

Lamp fonts or bases that fall into category 2 or 3 may at a later date be proven to have been made in the same mold. The validity of the similarities to some extent, hinges on the degree of perfection achieved in mold duplication in the 1860's and 1870's. Precise scientific measurement and a better understanding of mold duplication processes used, could strengthen attribution.

Once it is established that two fonts have been made in the same mold, then the potential exists for what I will call *sequential attribution*. Positive sequential attribution requires that the union of the font and base occurred at the same factory. This is determined by (a) lamps with their parts fused together before annealing, or (b) a patented method of connection which required especially molded glass parts, or a permanent attachment at the time of manufacture, achieved by the use of custom-made metal parts.

Two lamp fonts that have been made in the same mold may have been permanently attached by the manufacturer to two bases that have different designs, and perhaps made with different colors or types of glass. With positive identification, pursuing a logical sequence can provide proof that two very different pieces of glass were made at the same factory. If the manufacturer of one of those parts is known, the origin of the other parts is identified on the basis of sequential attribution.

Early composite lamps with font and base pegs cemented into a brass connector, were sometimes assembled at the glass company, and sometimes by a distributor or perhaps a retailer. Positive sequential attribution cannot apply to these lamps, but the study of many examples along with all available primary source material can establish a strong likelihood that certain lamps were made by a specific manufacturer, or in a particular region. Glass types, color, special techniques, cutting and surface decoration also play an important role in reinforcing relationships.

Today, in the absence of catalogue information, this is the only means by which many of the colored, cased and cut or decorated lamps may be attributed to the Midwest factories. The greatest potential for identifying such unattributed lamps lies in the comparison of examples that are positively attributed to Atterbury & Co., or to Hobbs, Brockunier & Company.

One of the first steps when comparing bases is to draw the outline of the bases on sheets of tracing paper. Place one sheet on top of the other and hold them against a window, or on a light table and then rotate the top one to make the comparison.

The fact that comparison of nine bases made by Hobbs, Brockunier & Company revealed that seven were made with a plunger having the same imperfections, indicates the odds of finding parts made in the same mold are very good. This seems plausible when production records show that approximately 2000 fonts per week could be produced from one mold.[1]

In addition to lamps or parts which are so similar that they may have been made in the same mold, there are other data that could be the basis of sequential attribution. These include:

Patented related lamps, particularly those that are patent dated and/or signed with the patentee's, assignee's or the manufacturer's name. This is very reliable but not infallible.

Molded handles are usually quite distinctive and may have been either patented, made in the same mold, or made by a specific company.

Applied or free-formed handles that exhibit distinctive manipulation may suggest a single glassmaker or the production of a specific factory or general area.

Marks made by tools used to affix applied handles to the body of a lamp, are usually a series of V's. These marks would be significant only if it could be proven they were made by the same tool. The most unusual mark that I have seen is the owl on the handle of a Central Glass Company lamp, shown on p. 102.

Design-related lamps are ones which were not made in the same mold but are entirely of the same design, or which have component parts that have the same design. They may be of different sizes. A design

relationship must not be considered conclusive evidence because some popular designs were made by several companies. On the other hand it is definitely worth noting as it is often this basic information that becomes the foundation for other observations and perhaps for reliable attributions.

Decoration-related lamps have surface decoration that may be attributed to an individual or a company. Comparison of actual examples with the use of a magnifying glass and in some instances scientific testing is needed to properly correlate the similarities.

The related lamps illustrated here can also be attributed to an area or company. Those with unusual glass can serve to identify other examples of glass vases, tableware and etc. made of the same glass. There are other examples in this book and in Oil Lamps I that relate to these lamps. The ones shown here were chosen because their relationships are more positive, or because after a certain point a group becomes unwieldy. Other related pairs and small groups are illustrated in the Composite and All Glass sections.

Caution must be exercised in the assessment and interpretation of all data. The foregoing observations are suggested avenues to explore; avenues that will likely dead-end short of the desired attribution. However, each established route may be reopened whenever new related information is discovered.

These lamps are not related! The four variations of the Waisted Broad Rib pattern, illustrate how common certain designs were; and how much they look alike at first glance. They were probably all made between 1865 and 1875 by different companies.

A Series

This first group of lamps, which I will call the "A" series, has as its anchor, one of two different bases illustrated and described in the Atterbury & Co. Pittsburgh, catalogues. To avoid confusion I will refer to the bases in this series as Baroque, a name occasionally used. All lamps illustrated here were likely made in the 1860's or early 70's. The Baroque bases are approximately the same size; 5-1/4" wide, measured from the centre point of each side, and 5-3/4" high.

a. Grant[ON] or Rand Rib
b. Cased and cut font, quatrefoil pattern
c. Painted font with gilt accents

d. Grant[ON] or Rand Rib font
e. & f. Filley[ON]
a. to e. Baroque bases

Baroque bases of the same size, from four different molds, are shown on the following pages with their sequentially related examples. All additional information known to me is recorded, and some tentative suggestions regarding origin, made. As new information is discovered, product and producer may be positively linked and a series of sequentially attributed lamps may be embraced.

Several fissures in the mold have left identical raised lines indicating bases (a) to (e) inclusive were made in the same mold. Base (a) is opaque and (b) to (e) are alabaster. There is no indication that (b), (c) or (d) were originally gilded. Fonts (a) in opaque white, and (d) in transparent green, do not have obvious identical mold characteristics and they are of only fair quality. This design is one of two patterns called Grant in the 1870's Atterbury & Co. catalogues; and was also discovered among fragments found at Sandwich, MS and at the site of the Mt. Washington Glass Works, in New Bedford, MS. I called it Rand Rib in OL I. As with examples of pressed and blown patterned tableware, some designs were made by more than one manufacturer and in both the East and the Midwest.

The cut design of font (b) has been well-executed. A major flaw, the broken bubble, did not discourage finishing this blank. Small bumps on the white surface indicate other bubbles. The font of lamp (c) has a painted design on opaque white glass. The fact that variations of this design have been seen on fonts with other shapes, suggests it was a popular type of decoration. Lamps (b) and (c) were illustrated in the Sandwich and Similar section in OL I. Nothing has been found that could positively attribute examples extant of these bases to Midwest factories, but the illustration in the Atterbury and Co. 1874 catalogue appears to be the same as (e), except for the threaded connector. It is the only example of this lamp illustrated in the known Atterbury catalogues. Although described as No. 40 base, it is clearly different from the other No. 40 bases they picture in their catalogues; and from the No. 40 marked bases. This is but one of the many questions still to be resolved that the Atterbury catalogues have provoked. Between the Atterbury brothers' patents and the company catalogues, there is however, the most complete record of production of a single manufacturer of lamps.

Filley fonts (e) and (f) each have two distinct, slightly raised circles 1/2" to 5/8" in diameter. These are below the ribbed band, approximately 1" and 1-1/4" to the left of the vertical mold mark. There is one smaller circle about 1/4" in diameter adjacent to one of the larger circles. Both fonts are of average quality, but the opalescent shoulder on the blue one places it in a very desirable category. I have seen one other example on a different base.

Collars on all are No. 2 and the heights are:
(a) 12-5/8", (b) 13", (c) 13-3/4", (d) 12-1/2", (e) 13-1/2" and (f) 11-3/4".

g. Engraved scene font with Baroque base
h. Engraved Swag and Tassel font with Baroque base

Imperfections establish that bases (g) and (h) are from the same mold. The fonts shown here, as well as the two on the next page, may have some relationship. All four appear to have been turned in the mold and the frosted areas of (g) and (a) on the next page were roughed on a lathe. Subject matter, rendition of trees — especially the crude tree trunks — and the quality and character of the engraving is similar on fonts (g) with the blue base; and (b) on the following page.

Although both bases are alabaster, the roughly textured exterior of the green one is likely caused by disintegration. The underside is smooth. The connector that is cemented to the pegs, also unscrews. These have been found on patented lamps made by Atterbury & Co. Pittsburgh, and by the New England Glass Company, Boston, as well as those made by the Boston & Sandwich Glass company. Both lamps have common early No. 2 collars.

Height of lamps: (g) 12-1/2" and (h) 13-1/2".

a. Cut font with spelter figural stem and iron base

b. Engraved scenic font, Griffin spelter stem, slate base

The fonts of lamps (a) and (b) are described on p. 21. Both figure stems are made of spelter. This was the common trade name for zinc, usually referred to today as white metal. It was cast in metal molds to create sculptural lamp parts that were usually gilded or finished to resemble bronze. Discovery and development of U.S. zinc mines in the early 1870's dramatically reduced foreign competition.[1] This probably led to the increase in variety and production of figure stem lamps that lasted through the 1880's.

Quality varied greatly, and although the original finishes are usually worn, repainted or re-gilded, it is still possible to find a lamp in almost perfect original condition. The example of the girl with a basket of flowers on her head and a bunch on her arm, has good detail; some of which may be partially obscured by a coat of gold paint. On lamp (b) the exceptionally fine detailing of the hair and feathers was revealed when layers of paint up to 1/8'' thick were removed from the Griffin.

Common early No. 2 collars are found on both lamps. Lamp (a) has an iron base and (b) has a slate base painted black. They were probably made between 1865 and 1875.

Height of lamps: (a) 14-1/2'' and (b) 14-1/4''.

The condition of the Baroque base, the quality of the glass and the cutting would all deduct points in the evaluation of this lamp. On the other hand, today the workmanship might be considered primitive and appropriate with the curdled cream texture of the opaque white casing. A large bubble at the neck is also visible.

There are several imperfections on the base; however they do not match any of the others in this series. The collar is a common early No. 2 size.

Height is: 13-3/4''.

c. White cased and cut font with opaque white gilt-decorated base

a. Flame Bullseye   b. Sherman[ON]   c. Sherman[ON]

d. Flame Bullseye   e. Early Moon and Star   f. Ring Punty, Sawtooth and Eye

The exceptional quality of these six lamps with pressed fonts, is their most obvious characteristic apart from the pattern relationships. It should always be kept in mind that sequential attribution of composite lamps cannot be positive, unless the combination is a type that required specific molding of the connecting parts. Other data that support an established relationship may indicate a high degree of probability.

Opaque lamp bases (a) and (b) have imperfections that indicate they are from the same mold. Fonts (a) and (d), Flame Bullseye, are made from identical molds, as indicated by the juxtaposition of pattern details. This also applies to fonts (b) and (c), Sherman.[ON 1] While the base (c) is similar to ones on p. 25, it is approximately 1/8'' wider. It is opaque, but with a transluscent outer surface or layer.

Bases (d), (e) and (f) required very careful scrutiny to substantiate the fact they were all made in the same mold. All were originally gilded in the same manner and feel exceptionally smooth to the touch. They are very thick and heavy and the one thinner portion of the black base appears bright ruby with strong back light, indicating an excess of ruby cullet or colorant.

Several years ago, I saw the Early Moon and Star font (e), combined with a bright amethyst No. 40 base.

Sizes are: (a) 13-1/4'', (b) 13-3/4'', (c) 12-1/4'', (d) 12'', (e) 11-1/2'', (f) 11''.

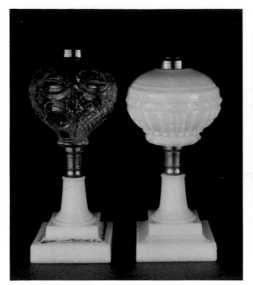

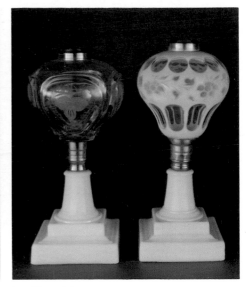

g. Cottage[ON] with Fleur-de-lis
h. Triple Flute and Bar

i. Triple Flute and Bar
j. Triple Flute and Bar

k. Quad Loop
l. Cased and Cut font

B Series

This "B" series compares lamps made in the 1860's and early 1870's. Both (g) and (h) have bases that appear to be identical, although there are no characteristics to provide absolute proof. They originally had the same gold bands including a narrow one near the bottom of the long stem section. Font (g) with worn gold decoration, was called Cottage in the Atterbury & Co. catalogue. Because they gave this name to two similar designs, I have chosen to differentiate by calling this one Cottage With Fleur-de-lis. All examples I have seen with the Fleur-de-lis have been pressed, and none has been combined with a base positively attributed to Atterbury

Other Triple Flute and Bar fonts are described in OL I, and are illustrated in both the Russell and Erwin Manufacturing Company hardware catalogue of 1865[1] and the Dietz & Company catalogue[2] of about the same time. All three of the examples here (h), (i) and (j), originally had gold bands, and (i) appears to have other gold or painted decoration on the side of the font. Its otherwise pristine condition demonstrates the appeal of gold decoration on the more expensive lamps. Font (h) is opaque and (i) and (j) are opalescent.

Again, two bases (k) and (l), appear to be the same, but without positive proof. They are 1/8" larger than (g) and (h) and not as white. Both fonts show restraint in design and execution. Neither the transluscent casing on (l) nor the rough cut and polished treatment is close to perfection, but the total effect is exceptional. Quad Loop (k), a design used by Hobbs, Brockunier & Company is, in my opinion, the finest example of a colorless pressed font I have seen. Another example of this font with the same engraving, has been seen combined with a bright green marked No. 40 base. These bases, apparently made in the East, are described on pp. 28-29.

Bases (m) and (n) appear to be identical, but lack conclusive evidence. They are not as wide as the other four on this page, and have slightly convex stems.

The design of fonts (m) and (o) is the same, except for the row of diamonds at the top of the pattern on the blown charcoal-tint Atterbury font. They called this pattern Chapman, so perhaps (m) should be called Chapman Without Diamonds.

The base on the Atterbury lamp with the screw connector is called Gem[ON]. All fonts on this page are pressed with the exception of (l) and (o).

Base widths: (g) and (h) 4-1/2", (k) and (l) 4-5/8", (m) and (n) 4-3/8".

Height of lamps: (g) 12", (h) 11-3/8", (i) 9-3/4", (j) 11", (k) 11-1/4", (l) 11-5/8", (m) 11-3/4", (n) 11-3/4", (o) 11-3/4".

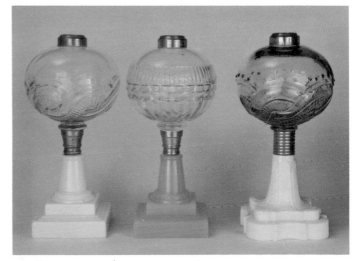

m. Chapman Without Diamonds
n. Chieftain[ON]
o. Chapman[ON] with Gem[ON] base.

a.& b. Beaded Bullseye
c. Shelley[ON]

d. Lily-of-the-Valley
   Dillaway Patent

e. Detail of font (a)

Dillaway

Hiram Dillaway, who was employed as head of the mold shop at the Boston & Sandwich Glass Company, obtained two patents for lamps in the 1870's. These are described in OL I, p. 115. There isn't a record of assignment or other information to link Dillaway lamps with Sandwich or other factories; therefore, while attribution to Sandwich seems logical, it is not positive.

The lamps on this page relate to Dillaway patent lamps. They may all have been produced by the same company that made Dillaway lamps.

Lamps (a), (b), (c) and (d) have mold-blown fonts engraved with the same design repeated three times. The rather crude workmanship suggests fast execution for mass production. Close examination reveals the likelihood that two of the lamps were engraved by the same person and the other two by a second engraver. Fonts (a) and (d), have flowers with longer outer petals and tendrils, that look like a scribble. This shows clearly in (e), the detail of font (a). A relationship is therefore established between (a) and the Lily-of-the-Valley font (d), with the Dillaway patent date July 18, 1871,[1] marked in the drip depression. The base of this lamp is opaque white with orange-painted trim.

Beaded Bullseye fonts (a) and (b) were made in the same mold. The pressed blue marble glass base is a No. 40 type described on p. 28. The engraved design on (b) and (c) has flowers with petals of the same length and tendrils that are better executed with the same flourish.

Shelley[ON] (c), has been found with many variations in size and number of beads, indicating that it was made by a number of companies.

f. Dillaway Patent lamp

g. Deer, Dog and Warrior

h. Deer, Dog and Warrior

The Dillaway patented lamp (f) is also illustrated and described in OL I, p. 115. Bases (f) and (g) appear to be identical but are without positive proof to indicate either the same or different molds. Fonts (g) and (h) were however made in the same mold.

These fonts comply with the description of ones

manufactured at the Mt. Washington Glass Works using a method introduced by Frederick S. Shirley, manager of the manufacturing department. Patent records[1] reveal that:

1. Lamps and glassware of this type, i.e. with bright lines and roughed on the outer surface, were made from March 1875 to at least 1880, at the Mt. Washington Glass Works.
2. Lamps of this type were described by Shirley as having been made by another lamp house in either 1876 or 1877.
3. The Bradley & Hubbard Manufacturing Company, West Meriden, CT, in a letter dated April 15, 1879, stated they bought "lamp pegs and founts" of this type from The Mt. Washington Glass Works, from March 1876 on and were still using them.

Frederick Shirley however, described the lamps sold to Bradley & Hubbard as: "These goods being for cheap lamps, the patterns were of set forms and bolder lines than intended to be used on finer work".

Fonts of this type are relatively common today. They are found with wide or with narrow lines on the composite lamps popular between 1875 and 1890. Study of more examples may yield additional clues to the attribution of these lamps.

A Deer, Dog and Warrior font appears on an iron base in an undated Avery Snell catalogue.[2] They have also been seen combined with two other iron bases. Sizes are: *(a)* 10", *(b)* 8-1/2", *(c)* 9-1/2", *(d)* approx. 9", *(e)* detail, *(f)* 9-1/4", *(g)* 9", *(h)* 9-1/8".

k. Bullseye and Fleur-de-lis with Sargent base
l. Honeycomb font with Sargent base
m. Sargent font and base

Patents often supply data of interest and/or importance to our knowledge of kerosene lamps. On March 4th, 1856, Prentice Sargent of Newburyport, MS obtained a patent for a rosin oil lamp. The patent drawing shows a handled lamp, however, an illustration of a Sargent patent lamp in *Early Lighting — A Pictorial Guide*, published by the Rushlight Club, shows a lamp with a plain font on a base like those above. A wide collar and a separation for an air intake between font and base were required characteristics for this patent. Although the wide-mouth all-glass lamp *(k)* could not have been used for Sargent's patent, it may have been used for a fuel other than kerosene. If No. 3 Jones kerosene burners were used, the lamps would appear today to have strange proportions.

Honeycomb *(l),* is a common pattern that is well documented in books on glass listed in the bibliography. There is nothing at the present time to link this lamp to a specific manufacturer. It is a deep purplish cobalt blue.

Lamp *(m),* much better proportioned, has a font that repeats the base design. To relate it to the patent, the pattern can be called Sargent.

Pressed bases *(k)* and *(l)* were made in the same mold. Sizes are: *(k)* 7-3/8", *(l)* 7-3/4", *(m)* 6-1/2".

i. Beaded Bullseye
j. Panelled Fern or Hammond

Only the pattern relates the Beaded Bullseye lamp *(i)* to the other examples. This unusual and attractive lamp has a pressed font with gilt decoration, combined with brass parts and a white glass base. The pressed glass bases *(i)* and *(j)* were substitutes for the common marble bases. The scarcity of glass bases used with brass stems, suggests they were either unpopular or poorly marketed.

An all-glass, mold-blown example of Panelled Fern or Hammond, as the pattern made at Sandwich is called, is shown in OL I, p. 103. Another mold-blown example is shown on p. 37.
Sizes are: *(i)* 12-1/4", *(j)* 8-7/8".

No. 40 bases

a. Reed[ON] or Single Icicle
b. California[ON] or Atterbury Loop

c. Wheeler[ON]   e. Ex[ON]
d. Decorated font   f. Grape Band

g. Prism   i. Chieftain[ON]
h. Diamond Cluster Panel   j. Panelled Bullseye

Catalogues confirm that three companies made No. 40 bases. The Cape Cod Glass Company at Sandwich, MS and the Mt. Washington Glass Works at New Bedford, MS listed them (see page 30). In the 1874 Atterbury & Co. catalogue, both the style of bases shown here, and Baroque bases, were illustrated, and described as No. 40.

The Baroque base with reeded stem, scalloped sides and notched corners, was shown in only a 5'' size. The No. 40 style pictured here, that is characterized by a panelled stem, flattened sides and rounded corners, was available in three sizes (widths): 3-1/4'', 3-3/4'' and 4-1/4''.

Cape Cod and Mt. Washington listed the sizes of their No. 40 bases as: 3-1/2'', 4'', 4-1/2'' and 5-1/2''. This suggests that the width of the bases may determine whether they were made in the East or the Midwest.

The Atterbury No. 40 bases, advertised in their 1874 catalogue, had the threaded pegs that were used with brass screw connectors, and although they described interchangeability as an advantage, specific combinations only were advertised. The Cape Cod and Mt. Washington companies sold fonts and bases separately and did not offer complete lamps. No doubt many of these, from the same manufacturer, were likely combined; but without additional supportive evidence, attribution to these companies should not be made on the basis of combinations found today. What is not documented about Atterbury & Co., is the design of most of their lamps before 1868, when they started using the screw connectors. Several of the patterned fonts which they combined with their patented connectors, are also found with common connectors and No. 40 bases. These patterns, named by Atterbury & Co. include: Chapman, Chieftain, Cottage, Grant, Ohio, Sherman and Tulip. Although these are original names used by Atterbury, other manufacturers could have given them different names. Mold-blown fonts were always used with threaded connectors, and some of these patterns were probably made by Atterbury before 1868. The pressed counterparts of these patterns may have been made by Atterbury, other Midwest companies or the New England companies.

The lamps illustrated here are grouped according to their markings and the width of their bases. Additional No. 40 bases are illustrated in this and the following section; and in OL I.

a. & b. Recently discovered original Atterbury names precede the common names. Both of these No. 40 bases are 3''. There appears to be a portion of the number 3 in one corner of the underside. Base (a), with a slight marbling of lighter blue, is remarkably similar to p. 26 (a). Base (b) is slightly transluscent. Sizes (a) 8-1/8'' and (b) 7-3/4''.
c. to f. All sizes of these unmarked bases are listed in the Atterbury catalogues and shown with threaded connectors. All have very good pattern definition.

Wheeler (c) is illustrated in OL I and in the Atterbury & Co. catalogues. The transluscent yellow-green base (d) is a rare shade. It was a strange choice to be combined with the painted and gilded opaque white font.

Ex *(e)* also in the Atterbury catalogues, was the common abbreviation for Excelsior, a name given to different patterns by other companies. This mold-blown font is of mediocre quality. Grape Band *(f)* described in greater detail in OL I is also mold-blown, but exceptionally well defined. The lavender base color is a thin layer over a greyish base. Similar ones are illustrated on page 41.

Lamps *(c)*, *(e)* and *(f)* are probably Midwest in origin. More information is needed to attribute *(d)*. Sizes are: *(c)* 8-5/8'', *(d)* 9-3/4'', *(c)* 10-3/4'', and *(f)* 9-3/4''.

g. to j. These No. 40 bases are marked on the underside: *(g)* 40 and 3-1/2, *(h)* 40 and 4, *(i)* 40 and 4-1/2 and *(j)* 40 and 5-1/2.

All these bases and fonts are of good to excellent quality. The green base *(g)* is transluscent and the Prism font blown. Gilded and slightly opalescent base *(h)* is combined with a pressed font that, while attractive, does not fit the connector very well. It may originally have been designed for an all-glass lamp. Base *(i)* also slightly opalescent, is combined with a pressed Chieftain font. Like those beside it, base *(j)* has an opaque, but lustrous quality, although this one is not opalescent. With the engraved Panelled Bullseye font, it is a tall and handsome lamp. Sizes are *(g)* 9-5/8'', *(h)* 9-1/2'', *(i)* 11-1/2'', and *(j)* 14-1/2''.

l. Blue cased and cut font mounted on a green transluscent base. The base is marked "40" in one corner and "5-1/2" in the other. Height is 13-3/16''
Courtesy, Sandwich Glass Museum, Sandwich Historical Society

k. This blown opalescent candlestick, with gilt floral decoration, is seated in a pewter socket or connector. The base with gilt bands is marked "40" in one corner and "4" in the other. Height is 12-3/4''
Courtesy, The Chrysler Museum Institute of Glass,
Gift of Walter P. Chrysler, Jr.

The Mt. Washington factory, when located in South Boston, and the Cape Cod factory could have been making No. 40 bases during most of the 1860's. Another possibility is that the same No. 40 base molds, were used by both companies. Cape Cod ceased operating in 1869, about the time Mt. Washington moved to New Bedford.

Kauko Kahila, Curator of Glass at the Sandwich Museum, has undertaken excavations at the Mt. Washington, New Bedford, MS factory site. He has compared the fragments he found with those from the Sandwich and other areas. Comparison of lamp fragments should be enlightening.

The exceptionally fine examples on this page have No. 40 marked bases. Their sizes and probable date of manufacture, circa 1865, indicate they were made at Sandwich, MS by the Cape Cod Glass Company.

LIST OF GLASS WARE.

CAPE COD GLASS COMPANY.

Medicine Squares.

No. 1, 6 oz. . . . .
" 2, 4 oz. . . . .
" 2, 4 oz. salt mouth, . .
" 3, 2 oz. . . . .
" 3, 2 oz. salt mouth, . .
" 4, 1 3-4 oz. saddle-bag, .
" 5, 1 oz. . . . .
" 6, 1½ oz. . . . .
(Stoppers ground in air tight.)

Sundries.

No. 56 French flute Celery, .
" 59 Bitter Bottle and tubes, .
Bird Boxes, . . .
Bird Baths, . . .
Enameled Nest Eggs, .
Round Lenses, (various sizes
Oval Lenses, . . .
5 Ribbed Deck Lights, .
7 " " .
8 " " .
Prism Conical Deck Lights,
3 sizes . . .
Sidewalk Lights, . .
Pickle Jars, . . .
Match Boxes, . . .
Flower Vases, (for painting)
Lantern Glasses, . .

Lamp Goods.

Lamp Feet (brass sockets.)

No. 1, 4 in. Square, . . .
" 2, 3 1-2 in. Square, . .
" 7, 3 1-2 in. Concave and reeded,
" 8, 4 in. Concave and reeded, .
" 40, 3 1-2 in. . . .
" 40, 4 in. . . .
" 40, 4 1-2 in. . . .
" 40, 5 1-2 in. . . .
(The above in various colors or gilt
if desired.)

Founts.

No. 39-2 A collars, . .
" 39-1 A collars . .
" 39-1 A collars and feeders, .
" 39-1 B collars, . .
" 39-1 B collars and feeders, .
" 91-1 Squat B collars, .
" 91-1 Squat B collars and feeders,
" 91-1 Tall B collars and feeders,
" 97-2 Sunflower A collars, .
" 97 Mammoth D collars and
feeders, . . .

Hand Lamps.

No. 24 Hotel-fluid, . .
" 37 Mellon, . . .
" 52 Ribbed (squat) . .

Hand Lamps.
CONTINUED.

" 83 Plain Concave, . .
" 97 Sunflower, . . .
" 200 Gaines, . . .
" 210 Ring, (small) . .
" Boston Beauty. . .

Chimnies.

No. 1 (B) . . . .
" 2 (A) . . . .
" 3 (E) . . . .
" 4 (F) . . . .
Sun, (blown) . . .
Sun, (mould) . . .
Light-House A (mould.) .

Pegs.

No. 19 Mirrors, . . .
" 31 Acorn, (vine) . .
" 37 Mellon, . . .
" 38-0 Morey, . . .
" 38-1 Morey, . . .
" 38-2 Morey, . . .
" 45 Star and punty, . .
" 58 Ring, . . .
" 61 Corduroy, . . .
" 81 Mitre, . . .
" 93-1 Punty and Groove, .
" 93-0 Punty and Groove, .
" 94-1 Rose Leaf, . .
" 97-1 Sunflower, . .
" 97-0 Sunflower, . .
" 115-1 Howard, . . .
" 115-0 Howard, . . .
" 116-1 Sunflower and reeded, .
Mt. Washington No. 1. .
" No. 2. .
" 301 Cut and engraved, .
" 302 " " .
" 303 " " .
" 304 " " .
" 38-0 " " .
" 38-1 " " .
" 38-2 " " .
" 97-0 " " .
" 97-1 " " .

Plated Wares.

Plated Castors, Cake Baskets, Tea Sets, Ice Pitchers, Butters, Salts, Dishes, Molasses Pitchers, &c., &c., for Hotels, Restaurants, Families or other use.

Private Moulds.

Parties owning Moulds for Lantern Globes, Sidewalk Lights, Lenses, Bottles, &c., &c., can rely on our working them as reasonable as any one in the market.

Courtesy, Sandwich Glass Museum, Sandwich Historical Society

Mt. Washington GLASS WORKS,

FOUNTS.

No.			
1 B	Collar		$2.50
2 A	"		1.50
4 B	"		2.50
5 B	"	and feeder	2.25
6 A	"		1.12
7 D	"	and feeder	4.50
8 D	"		5.00
9 B	"	and feeder	2.25

Patent Founts in all patterns from $3.00 per doz. upwards.

HAND LAMPS.

No. 1,	Blown	$2.50
2,	"	2.00
Washington		1.25
Boston Beauty		1.00
No. 1,	Flint	1.75
1½,		1.25
2,	National	1.00
3,		.90
3,	Concave	1.20
4,		1.12
5,		1.00
1,	Monitor	1.75
2,		1.30

STAND LAMPS,
Great variety, Plain and Decorated.
From $2.00 to $40.00 per dozen.

Blown, Pressed, Cut and Decorated Pegs.
Large assortment, from 60 Cents to $10.00 per dozen.

OPAL LAMP FEET, PLAIN AND DECORATED.

	Plain.		Dec'd Gilt.		Dec'd Flowers.	
Octagon.	3½ in.	$1.50	3½ in.	$4.50	3½ in.	$4.50
	4 in.	2.00	4 in.	5.50	4 in.	5.50
	4½ in.	3.75	4½ in.	8.00	4½ in.	8.00
	5 in.	5.00	5 in.	10.00	5 in.	10.00
N. R.	3 in.	$1.10	3 in.	$4.00	3 in.	$4.00
	3½ in.	1.25	3½ in.	4.75	3½ in.	4.75
	4 in.	1.50	4 in.	5.25	4 in.	5.25
	5 in.	2.75	5 in.	6.00	5 in.	7.00
Mt. Wash.	3½ in.	$1.10	3½ in.	$4.75	3½ in.	$4.25
Concave	4 in.	1.62½	4 in.	5.00	4 in.	5.00
	5 in.	4.00	5 in.	7.50	5 in.	7.50
Square.	3 in.	$1.15	3 in.	$4.00	3 in.	$4.00
	3½ in.	1.40	3½ in.	4.60	3½ in.	4.60
	4 in.	1.75	4 in.	5.25	4 in.	5.25
	4½ in.	2.50	4½ in.	7.00	4½ in.	7.00
No. 40.	3½ in.	$1.40	3½ in.	$4.30	3½ in.	$4.30
	4 in.	1.75	4 in.	5.40	4 in.	5.40
	4½ in.	3.50	4½ in.	7.50	4½ in.	7.50
	5½ in.	5.50	5½ in.	9.50	5½ in.	9.50

PATENT FEET, PLAIN AND DECORATED.
From $3.00 per dozen upward.

The information revealed in catalogues and price lists gives an insight into lamp manufacture and marketing. Although this material often provides attribution and dating for examples extant, it sometimes provokes questions. The information revealed here may be compared with that in other catalogues of the same period, especially those starting on p. 146, as well as the Southlands catalogue pages reproduced in OL I.

Deming Jarves left the Boston & Sandwich Manufacturing Co. that he founded in 1826, to start the Cape Cod Glass Company. This company, also located in Sandwich MS, operated from 1859 to 1869 when Jarves died.

Mt. Washington Price List c. 1870-1875 from private collection

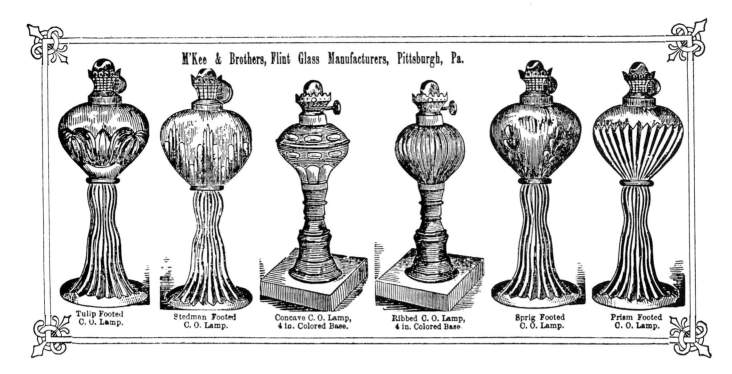

M'Kee & Brothers, Flint Glass Manufacturers, Pittsburgh, Pa.

Tulip Footed C. O. Lamp.   Stedman Footed C. O. Lamp.   Concave C. O. Lamp, 4 in. Colored Base.   Ribbed C. O. Lamp, 4 in. Colored Base.   Sprig Footed C. O. Lamp.   Prism Footed C. O. Lamp.

CARBON OIL LAMPS.

Pressed Assorted Large Pegs, Ellipse, Star, Concave, Chain, Gaines, Cincinnati, Shell, Prism, Stedman, Tulip, Sprig, Vine..per doz. $2 75

Pressed R. L. Footed Lamps, no Burner...............	"	4 00
Pressed Argus Footed Lamps, no Burner...............	"	4 00
Pressed Concave Footed Lamps, no Burner...........	"	4 00
Pressed Ring Footed Lamps, no Burner................	"	3 50
Pressed Ribbed Footed Lamps, no Burner...........	"	3 50
Pressed Large Suspension Fount, No. 1 or No. 2 Mouths....	"	4 00
Pressed Small Suspension Fount, No. 1 Mouth..............	"	3 00
Pressed 4 inch White Base and Stem.................	"	4 50
Pressed 4 inch Black Base and Stem.................	"	4 25
Pressed 5 inch White Base and Stem.................	"	6 00
Pressed 5 inch Black Base and Stem.................	"	5 50
Pressed Ring Hand Lamp, no Burner..............	"	2 33
Pressed Ribbed Hand Lamp, no Burner..............	"	2 33

BACON'S BURNERS (for burning without Chimneys), will be substituted at same price when desired.

❦

The Mt. Washington Glass Works was also established by Deming Jarves. Founded in 1837 in South Boston, it later moved to New Bedford, MS in 1869.[1]

The 1864 M'Kee illustrations and price lists reproduced here are from a collection of five recently reprinted M'Kee catalogues.[2] The all-glass lamps illustrated in more than one of their catalogues must have had substantial production and yet they are surprisingly rare today. The company was located in Pittsburgh. Each of these companies was considered a prominent glass manufacturer in its time; and is recognized as such today.

Identifying patterns by the names listed will provide an ongoing and probably unending search. The No. 1, No. 2 and No. 40 bases undoubtedly relate to those illustrated in this section. Could the Cape Cod Corduroy pattern be the same as the Reed Oval fonts, combined with No. 1 bases? M'Kee's Concave is clearly the pattern called Ring Punty, or R & P in the Fellows, Hoffman & Co. catalogue. (see pp. 146-147) As new information becomes available the interpretation of existing knowledge will be altered.

CARBON OIL LAMPS.

Pressed Ring Hand.....................................per doz.	$4	75
Pressed Ring Footed.............................. "	5	75
Pressed Ribbed Footed.......................... "	5	75
Pressed Ribbed Hand............................ "	4	75
Pressed Argus Footed........................... "	6	25
Pressed Concave Footed........................ "	6	25
Pressed R. L. Footed............................. "	6	25
Pressed Shell Footed............................. "	7	25
Pressed Sprig Footed............................. "	7	25
Pressed Tulip Footed............................. "	7	25
Pressed Vine Footed.............................. "	7	25
Pressed Stedman Footed........................ "	7	25
Pressed Prism Footed............................ "	7	25
Pressed Ring 4 inch Colored Base............ "	8	50
Pressed Ribbed, 4 inch Colored Base....... "	8	50
Pressed Turnip, 4 inch Colored Base........ "	8	50
Pressed R. L. 4 inch Colored Base........... "	8	50
Pressed Argus, 4 inch Colored Base......... "	8	50
Pressed Concave, 4 inch Colored Base...... "	8	50
Pressed Shell, 5 inch Colored Base.......... "	11	00
Pressed Sprig, 5 inch Colored Base.......... "	11	00
Pressed Tulip, 5 inch Colored Base.......... "	11	00
Pressed Vine, 5 inch Colored Base........... "	11	00
Pressed Stedman, 5 inch Colored Base...... "	11	00
Pressed 3½ inch White Base and Stem....... "	4	00
Pressed 3½ inch Black Base and Stem....... "	3	50
Pressed Prism, 5 inch Colored Base.......... "	11	00
Pressed large Suspension Fountain, No. 1 Burners........... "	6	50
Pressed large Suspension Fountain, No. 2 Burners........... "	11	00
Pressed small Suspension Fountain, No. 1 Burners........... "	5	25
Large Harps for Hanging Lamps, Bronzed....... "	4	00
Small Harps for Hanging Lamps, Bronzed....... "	4	00
Small Side Brackets and Reflectors............. "	5	00
Large Side Brackets and Reflectors............. "	5	00
Pressed Ellipse C. O. Lamps, 5 inch Colored Base............ "	11	00
Pressed Star and Concave Lamps, 5 inch Colored Base....... "	11	00
Pressed Chain Lamps, 5 inch Colored Base..... "	11	00
Pressed Gaines Lamps, 5 inch Colored Base..... "	11	00
Pressed Cincinnati Lamps, 5 inch Colored Base.............. "	11	00
Pressed Assorted Small Pegs, R. L. Concave and Argus..... "	1	75
Pressed Assorted Small Pegs, Ribbed and Ring..... "	1	70

Courtesy, The Corning Museum of Glass, Corning, New York

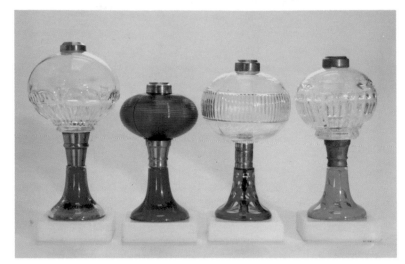

a. Heart-Top Panel with transfer and painted stem on opaque white base.
b. Reed Oval font with base as above only (M-1).
c. Rib Band font, (see OL I) cased stem, blue cut to clear.
d. Triple Flute and Bar. (See p. 34 and OL I for others) Opalescent off-white base. *Courtesy, Huntington Galleries.*

e. Reed Oval font in opaque white. Black base (M-1).
f. Reed Oval font in cranberry. Black base with fluted stem (M-1).
g. Ring Punty and Heart. (See OL I) Black base with ground corners (M-1).
h. Ring Punty with opaque white base (M-1).

i. Reed Oval font; brass stem, marble base.
j. Reed Oval font; brass stem, marble base.
k. Reed Pear font, green with white threads; opaque white base.
l. Reed Pear font, cranberry with white threads; brass stem, marble base.

No. 1 & 2 bases

All the lamps on this and the next two pages are marked, or related to marked examples. Bases that are embossed with a number 1 or 2 on the underside, are noted as (M-1) or (M-2) in the captions. Those marked 1 are 4'' wide, and those marked 2 are 3-1/2'' wide. Some of these may be the No. 1 and No. 2 bases mentioned in the Cape Cod and Mt. Washington price lists. (see pp. 30-31) Four different designs are included.

Certainly, the most unusual base is the one with the mold-blown stem and pressed base with a hole in the center. *(detail 1)* All but one of these were glued together with an evidently excellent adhesive. Some of the connectors are very unusual.

Atterbury & Co. named three different lamps Reed, including their oval-shaped ribbed font, similar to those

illustrated here. They do not illustrate a ribbed pear shape. I will use the names, Reed Oval and Reed Pear, for these mold-blown fonts. It is possible that several companies made these designs.

Detail 1. Detail of bases *(a)* to *(d)*.

All the colored Reed Oval lamps on this page were made in the same mold. Readily detected flaws determined this. The blown ribbed design transforms the twisted, or spiralled white glass threads, into a zig-zag effect. The pear-shaped ribbed fonts, *(k)* and *(l)*, and those on p. 34, are each from a different mold.

All the colorless fonts *(a)* to *(h)* are shown combined with other bases elsewhere in this book and in OL I. Triple Flute and Bar *(d)*, and *(a)* on p. 34, is a common early design. Several examples are shown in OL I. Reed Oval lamps are relatively common. The Chrysler Museum has a blue Reed Oval font with white threads. Its unmarked base is otherwise a white counterpart of *(o)*, opposite.

Detail 2. Yellow is the rarest color in the Reed Oval threaded font.

Sizes are:
(a) 10-1/2'', *(b)* 8-1/8'',
(c) 9-1/2'', *(d)* 9-5/8'',
(e) 8-1/4'', *(f)* 8-1/4'',
(g) 9-1/2'', *(h)* 9-1/2'',
(i) 7-3/4'', *(j)* 7-7/8'',
(k) 8-5/8'', *(l)* 8-1/2''.

Opposite ▷

m. Green alabaster font. Cased green cut to clear stem with white base. (Not available to examine for mark).
n. Cased cranberry or ruby cut to clear font. Opaque white base (M-1).
o. Reed Oval font. Cranberry or red with white threads. Opaque black base (M-1).
p. Reed Oval font, blue with white threads. Marbled, multi-colored painted stem; white unmarked base.

These lamps are all approximately 8'' high.

m.

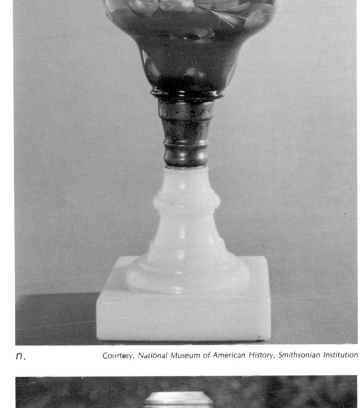

n.

o.

p.

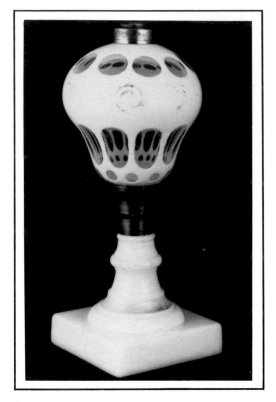

b. White cased and cut to clear font, with opaque white base (M-1)

Unfortunately this well-proportioned lamp has worn gilding. Originally the scrolled design on the font, and the bands on the base, would have considerably enhanced its appearance.

Mold-blown fonts (c), (d), (e) and (f) do not have any identical mold characteristics in common with others of the same size and design shown on pp. 32 and 33.

c. d. e. & f.

c. Reed Pear font. Colorless font with slightly opalescent less dense white base (M-2).
d. Reed Pear font with scalloped base.
e. Reed Oval font with slightly marbelized opalescent and dense transluscent glass.
f. Reed Oval font with scalloped base.

All these lamps appear to be from the late 1860's or early 70's.

Sizes are: (a) 15-3/16'', (b) 10-1/4'', (c) 8-1/2'', (d) 7'', (e) 7-3/4'', (f) 6-3/8''.

Courtesy, The Chrysler Museum Institute of Glass, Gift of Walter P. Chrysler, Jr.

a. Triple Flute and Bar (M-2). see p. 32

This second example of the popular 1860's pattern is combined with a No. 2, 3-1/2'' base, having a slightly concave fluted stem that is similar to, but not the same as (f) on p.32. It is attributed to the Cape Cod Glass Company.

g. & h.

i.

j.

k.

fig. 1 Detail of
Cup Connector.

g. Ring Punty, Concave^ON or R&P^ON with fluted stem.

h. Ring Punty, Concave^ON or R&P^ON with Panelled Teardrop stem.

i. Disassembled lamp showing the unusual stem used in these lamps.

j. Cable and Dart with fluted stem.

k. Silvered glass lamp with vintage engraving.

Cup Connector

Two unusual features are common to all lamps on this page. One is the cup-shaped connector, (fig. 1), with less than a 1/4'' metal band visible; and the other is the type of mold-blown stem that is almost closed at the bottom.

Neither the fonts of (g), (h) or (i), nor any of the stems, have distinctive marks that prove or disprove they were made in the same molds. The excellent quality pressed Ring Punty fonts were definitely made in molds that were different from those used to make any similar fonts pictured in OL I, or among those I have been able to examine for this book.[1]

Concave and R&P are both original names for this pattern. See pp. 30 and 31.

The good quality white fluted stems are superior to the greyish toned glass Teardrop Panel stems, which have obvious pieces of unmelted cullet. While the iron base (g) is a type associated with lamps circa 1870, all other

parts appear to be from the late 1850's or early 60's. This could indicate later assembly or a replacement. Slate bases (h), (i) and (j) were painted to resemble marble and stone. Both font and stem of Cable and Dart are fiery opalescent. Sizes are (g) 8-5/8'', (h) 8-3/8'', (i) 8-5/8'', (j) 8-3/4''.

The design of the white fluted stems (g) and the silvered one (k) is the same. A chemical analysis has determined that this is a silvered rather than mercury glass lamp.[2] Today there are fewer than six known examples of silvered lamps of the late 1850's and early 1860's and none of the others has a fluted stem and marble base. This lamp, (except for the pewter connector and collar) comes close to the S.E. Southlands 1859 catalogue description of: ''No. 589 Engraved Silvered Glass Fount 37.50 (per dozen)''. It was further described as having a White Marble, 5'' Square Base, Silvered Fluted Glass Column and 12'' high. Southlands measurements included the burner. Lamp (k), including the burner, is 12-1/2'' high. The Boston Silver Glass Company is reported to have made this type of glass in the late 1850's and 1860's.[3]

The unmarked cast pewter burner with brass domed deflector was found in the same general area as the lamp. It has a wide thread typical of pewter pre-kerosene burners. The double-walled sealed font has protected the silvered coating whereas it has deteriorated on the interior of the stem. The design of these stems with a small aperture for the bolt at the bottom, would lend itself to a very good seal. Silvered and sealed curtain tiebacks with similar vintage engraving were popular during the 1850's and 60's.

a. Blocked Fern. Gem base
b. Festoon.ON Semi-circle Rib and Jewel. Gem with Leaf Base
c. Diamond Cluster and Rib. Gem base
d. Gem base

e. Scalloped Rib Band. Atterbury Gem base
f. Scalloped Rib Band. Gem base
g. Loop and Dart and Heart. Gem base
h. Scalloped Rib Band. Gem base

i. Chieftain.ON No. 40 base
j. Chieftain.ON No. 40 base
k. Chieftain.ON Baroque base
l. Grant.ON Baroque base

C Series

Experimentation with glass formulas and manufacturing techniques, and the unique results of hand finishing, are important characteristics of the art glass movement that began in the 1880's and flourished for several decades. In the 1860's many lamps were made with art glass characteristics and these could be referred to as early art glass. The glass shown here is unusual and rare. Its use for lamp bases that can be related and dated, permits reliable identification. Although it would appear that most, if not all of these lamps, were made by Atterbury & Co., or originated in the Midwest, I think more evidence is needed before making a positive attribution which would include every lamp.

Gem was the name Atterbury & Co. gave to the base (e). The other similar bases shown on this and the opposite page, have easily recognizable variations, apart from the obvious screw connector and the scallops terminating the panels near the top of the stem. There are leaves on the four corners of base (a) on this page and on all bases on the page opposite. Some have a rib or protrusion, more or less defined, about 3/16'' above the bottom, and (d) has an extra step. Mold or plunger defects, or design characteristics indicate the following bases or fonts were made in the same mold:

Bases (a) (b) (c) and (d)
Bases (g) and (h)
Bases (k) and (l)
Bases (m) (n) and (o)
Fonts (e) not threaded, (f) and (h)
Fonts (i) (j) and (k).

Several of these and similar lamps are illustrated in OL I. Fonts (m) and (o) are pressed. All others are mold-blown, except (c), which is undetermined. I haven't any reason to doubt that the font (c) was made in America, but its unusual shape closely resembles lamps in foreign catalogues.

The marbled coloration and strange pearly sheen on bases (c) and (d), appear to be vitreous, but the color does not penetrate beyond about 1/64''. Chipped parts, that seem to have flaked off at the top of the stem, reveal an inner core with a solid color that is lighter than, but related to, the exterior. Either layers of two different types of glass, or a heat sensitive formula, has been suggested as the cause of this condition. The other marbled bases illustrated here do not seem to have this inner core.

The Atterbury Gem base (e), is a riot of color, ranging from pale turquoise through blood red to blue and purple. A smaller example is illustrated in OL I, p. 143.

m. Heart-Top Panel.   *n.* Panelled Fern or Hammond   *o.* Bullseye Band Entwined
All bases are Gem with Leaf, pressed in the same mold

No. 40 base *(i)* ranges from cloudy transluscent to almost clear transparent. Both *(i)* and *(j)* are 4-1/4'' wide, a size made by Atterbury & Co. The Baroque base *(k)*, while slightly marbled, would be better described as shaded from medium blue to dark brown; almost black. Whether intended or accidental, the result is excellent. From the same mold, *(l)* is a cloudy shade of green; very different from other lamp bases.

Although the bases *(m)*, *(n)* and *(o)* are from the same mold, the fonts are not related. The

Panelled Fern pattern *(n)*, (shown also on p. 27) is mold-blown, and the other two fonts are pressed. The base *(n)* has a most unusual color combination, shading from green to maroon. The undersides of bases often reveal surprising color differences.

Sizes are: *(a)* 8-5/8'', *(b)* 8-5/8'', *(c)* 7-7/8'', *(d)* base only, *(e)* 10-3/8'', *(f)* 10-3/8'', *(g)* 10-5/8'', *(h)* 10-3/4'', *(i)* 10-3/4'', *(j)* 10-1/2'', *(k)* 10-3/4'' *(l)* 9-1/2'', *(m)* 10-3/4'', *(n)* 10-1/2'', *(o)* 10-3/4''.

Iden & Co.

fig. 1 A gala party, depicting earlier times, pictures the Iden & Co. showroom at 194 & 196 Hester St., New York.
Trade card, original size 3-1/4'' x 4-1/2''. 1871. Schumacher & Ettlinger Litho, N.Y. *Courtesy, Wm. Frost Mobley.*

a. A fine quality spelter figural lamp, with original antique bronze finish in exceptional condition. The roughed and cut font, signed J.F. IDEN, is enclosed in a metal holder with oval windows. There is a Greek key design on the shoulder. Probably made between 1865 and 1870. Height is 14''.

Lamps marked J. F. IDEN N.Y. have been found in several different designs. Most of them are marked in the bottom of the font where the name can only be detected by peering through the collar. This explains why so few have been identified. One of these lamps, pictured in OL I, appeared to read J. FIDEN, but study of other examples has revealed that the correct name is J.F. IDEN.

New York City directories trace the Idens connected with lamps and lighting. The listings for years ending on May 1st, reveal that Henrich Iden, whose name appeared later as Henry, was listed in 1854 as a cabinetmaker residing at 60 Elm. In 1856 his address changed to 194 Hester. Subsequent listings note changes and additions.

May 1, 1859	Iden, Henry, Cabinetmaker 194 Hester, h 192 Hester Iden, John F. Metalspinner 137 Elm, h 142 Elm
May 1, 1865	Iden, Henry, furniture 194 Hester, h 192 Hester Iden, John F. lamps 137 Elm, h 187 Elm
May 1, 1867	Iden, Henry, lamps, 196 Hester, h E. 83d N Av. A Iden, John F. lamps, 196 Hester, h 165 83d Iden & Co. lamps, 196 Hester
May 1, 1868	Iden, Henry, fixtures, 194 Hester, h E. 83d n First av. Iden, John F., fixtures, 194 Hester, h E 83d n Third av. Iden & Co. fixtures, 194 Hester
May 1, 1870	Iden, Henry, fixtures 196 Hester, h E. 83d N Av. A Iden, John F., fixtures 196 Hester, h 16 E. 83rd Iden & Co., fixtures 129 Baxter & 196 Hester
May 1, 1872	Iden, Henry, chandeliers, 196 Hester, h 423 E. 83d Iden, John F., chandeliers, 196 Hester, h 236 E. 83d Iden & Co. chandeliers, 196 Hester

After 1876, only a home address is given for John F. Iden.

May 1, 1878	Iden, Henry, Chandeliers, 194 Hester, h 423 E. 83d Iden, Henry jr. fixtures, 194 Hester, h 158 Bowery Iden, John F. h 288 E. 83d. Iden & Co., chandeliers, 194 Hester
May 1, 1888	Iden, Charles W. fixtures, University pl. c E. 9th, h 57 Christopher Iden, Henry, fixtures, University pl. c E. 9th, h 119 E. 17th Iden, Henry jr. fixtures, University pl. c E. 9th, h 38 E. 4th Iden & Co. fixtures, University pl. c E 9th

This is the first record of a Charles Iden connected with the firm.

In 1892 Henry, Henry Jr. and Charles were still listed as associated with Iden & Co., which was then described as manufacturers of gas fixtures and electroliers, located at 26 University Place. In that same year, Mary C. Iden was listed as the widow of John F. Iden.

In 1906, the Acetylene Lamp Co., 50 University Place, New York, and also Montreal, Canada, advertised the Beck-Iden lamp.

The Iden lamps opposite, are excellent examples to illustrate the complexities of attribution. Some of their cast spelter parts were made in the same mold; and their frosted glass inserts are all embossed on the bottom, J.F. IDEN N.Y.

Lamps (c) and (d) are also illustrated in the Dietz catalogue circa 1865, and in the Boston & Sandwich catalogue of the same period. These companies, who describe themselves as manufacturers, both gave the number 23 to this lamp, and the number 22, to its all-metal counterpart. The Sandwich catalogue also describes this lamp

c. & d. Pair of two-part brass and spelter lamps with glass fonts signed J.F. IDEN N.Y.

b. Two-part brass and spelter lamp with roughed and cut font, signed J.F. IDEN N.Y.

as French. This could mean, it was made in France; was in the French style; or was finished in French bronze, (as some spelter articles were advertised.)

The Dietz & Co. catalogue, on the same plate, illustrates a lamp with a stem and base like *(b)*, a different platform, and a font with an engraved design. Dietz also offered separate bases and stems. Two examples of the stem and base combination *(b)* have been seen with Ripley Wedding Lamp fonts.

The base portion of *(b)* below the stem, was made in the same mold as *(d)*. The other base *(c)*, from a different mold, has a pronounced mold mark in the center of each face and corner.

It is evident that both companies sold

these lamps. The Boston & Sandwich company probably made the fonts. But who made the rather crudely cast metal parts? It could have been Dietz, although, their bronze castings are of better quality. It could have been J.F. Iden; or the parts may have been imported from France. This style, with a separate stand to hold the font, was commonly used in Europe for both Carcel and kerosene lamps. Other typically European lamps are illustrated in the Russell and Erwin catalogue (see pp. 148-151). The term ''Sold by'' is a safe way to describe these lamps. If they *are* to be attributed, it is important to include all companies involved. Sizes are: *(b)* approx. 14'', *(c)* 14-3/8'', *(d)* 14-3/8''.

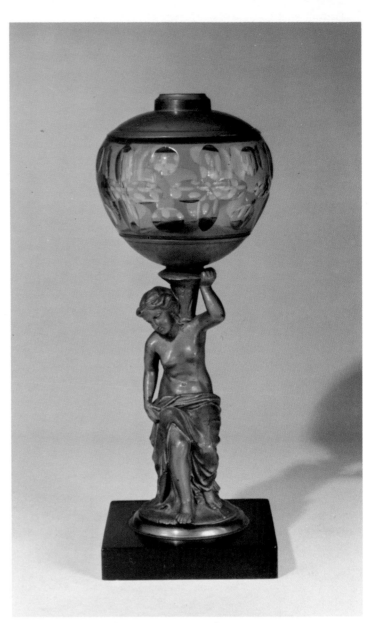

a. Composite lamp signed J.F. IDEN N.Y. Height is 13-1/4''

b. Figural lamp signed J.F. IDEN N.Y. Height is 14-3/4''

c. Plain green glass font signed, J.F. IDEN N.Y. Height is approx. 10''

d. Detail of stippled pattern on pressed base of composite lamp (a) shown above

Since the foregoing indicates a relationship between Iden & Co. and the Boston & Sandwich Manufacturing Company, it is likely the latter made these cased and cut fonts, embossed, J.F. IDEN N.Y. on the bottom.

Unfortunately the font of (a) has been altered. The brass shoulder has been cut off around the collar, and the brass part at the bottom of the font would have been like that on (b). This may not be an original font and base combination. The style of this base marked, PAT APLD FOR, is similar in general construction to patented bases circa 1880. Although the scalloped skirt is only slightly opalescent, the effect is enhanced because it overhangs the blue hollow stem. This, combined with the stippled patterned base (d), suggestive of earlier lacy glass; and the unusual shape, create a strikingly different lamp.

The copper-bronze finish, on the brass and spelter parts of the figural lamp (b), is probably original. The base is slate. Lamp (c) circa 1880, has a green glass font embossed, J.F. IDEN N.Y. and an iron base. With such a long history of lamp production, and the markings described, many other examples of lamps manufactured or sold by Iden & Co. may be found.

Hearts

Hearts and Stars must have been a popular pattern between 1865 and 1875. It seems quite possible that Atterbury & Co. made this pattern. Hobbs, Brockunier & Company, Wheeling, WV used it with their patented connector, and the Central Glass Company, also in Wheeling, showed an all-glass version in their catalogue. These pages illustrate lamps that are related to Hearts and Stars; and point out some subtle differences in proportion and detail. Some relationships are vague and need additional examples for comparison. Several of these lamps are also illustrated in OL I.

Fonts (a), (b), (c), and (d) were all made in the same mold. This particular design lends itself to comparison. The size of the stars, the size and number of the diamonds, and the juxtaposition of these elements, are quite varied among the examples shown here and on the next page. The rather squared, or jowly appearance of these fonts, is an obvious common characteristic. The hearts are relatively small, and the diamonds within a mitred form, are relatively large. Both the quality, and color or tint of the fonts, vary considerably. The design of base (a), is one that was originally combined with an Atterbury 1862 patented font. Both bases (b) and (c) may have been made in the same mold, however, there is nothing obvious to prove or disprove this. Base (b) is transparent but slightly cloudy; while (c) is more cloudy and transluscent. The No. 40 base (d), is unmarked. It is just slightly under 3-3/4'' wide at its widest point, which is the size of the Atterbury No. 40 bases, rather than a No. 40 base size made in the East. These are remarkable similarities and coincidences, however, there is nothing that positively links lamps (a) to (d), with lamps (e) to (i).

Although the No. 40 base (d), is the same size as those on lamps (e) to (i), and has a lavender color or tint, it was not made in the same mold.

Lamp (e) has an unusual pattern that looks like hairpins. Fonts (f), (g), (h) and (i) are designs that were made by Atterbury. Bases (e) to (i), with variations in tint and transparency, all have identical, partially obscured marks on the underside, that appear to indicate the 3-3/4'' width made by Atterbury & Co.

The lavender color, or tint, on some of the opaque bases on this page, occurs only on the outer surface. When the underside is examined, it can be seen that the balance of the glass has a color that would not be very attractive if used for lamp bases. Some of this glass is streaked, some yellowish, and other examples are quite grey. The lavender color may have been brought out while reheating the bases; perhaps as a solution to utilizing a lesser quality glass or cullet. Lamps (j) and (k), with bases from the same mold, relate only to the others on this page because of their lavender coloration.

Sizes are: (a) 9-3/4'', (b) 9-1/2'', (c) 9-1/4'', (d) 9-1/4'', (e) 9'', (f) 8-3/4'', (g) 8-1/4'', (h) 9'', (i) 9-1/2'', (j) 8-1/2'', (k) 9-1/4''.

a. b. c. & d. Hearts and Stars fonts combined with various bases

e. Hairpins f. Lace[ON] or James g. Plain font h. Prism[ON] i. Tulip[ON]

j. Filley[ON] k. Lattice Band and Rib

a. b. & c. Hearts and Stars

d. & e. Hearts and Stars

f. Hearts and Stars   *g.* Eyes and Ties

h. i. & j. Hearts and Bars

Hobbs, Brockunier & Company made lamp *(a)* with a clinched connector. Although fonts *(a)*, *(b)* and *(c)* are almost the same size, and have proportionately much larger stars, there are definite differences, particularly in the sawtooth portion of the design.

Lamps *(b)* and *(e)* appear to be the ones illustrated in the Central Glass Company catalogue.[1] Like *(a)*, the stars on *(c)* are very large. Pattern definition on *(c)* is the clearest of all the examples shown here. The Hobbs simple Cloverleaf base *(d)*, is a better choice than the Blackberry base *(a)*, for such a busy patterned font. Fonts *(d)* and *(e)*, although similar to *(a)* to *(d)* on the preceding page, have much smaller diamonds.

The Hearts and Stars font *(f)*, is very similar in overall shape to Eyes and Ties *(g)*. Both have a very flat shoulder. The bases of these two lamps were made in the same mold, and are smaller examples of the shaded blue base shown in the section on composite lamps. It appears that these two lamps were patterns of another company or another mold maker.

The designer of Hearts and Bars *(h)*, *(i)* and *(j)*, has substituted bars for stars. Otherwise the pattern is the same. Fonts *(i)* and *(j)* were made in the same mold, and have smaller diamonds than those on example *(h)*. The bases of *(i)* and *(j)*, while similar, have distinct differences. On base *(i)*, each panel of the stem has a single raised rib, and the base of the stem is scalloped. Both bases have a diagonal rib pressed on the underside; but in the cobalt blue example *(j)*, this band is much narrower.

All of the hearts and related lamps shown here, have mold-blown fonts. With the exception of *(i)*, with a Taplin-Brown patent-dated collar,[2] and the replacement collar *(p. 41-d)*, all have collars of the type made before 1876. It would appear that all of these lamps were made in the Midwest.

Sizes are: *(a)* 10″, *(b)* 8-1/2″, *(c)* 8-3/4″, *(d)* 9-1/2″, *(e)* 7-3/4″, *(f)* 10-1/4″, *(g)* 10-1/4″, *(h)* 10″, *(i)* 9″, *(j)* 9-1/4″.

a. Nosegay with ribbed base

b. Plain font with Stippled Fishscale base

c. Nosegay font with Stippled Fishscale base

New Martinsville

Sequential attribution relates all of the lamps on this page. Their related characteristics are evident on all lamps except Hanson (f), which has the same pressed pattern on the underside of the base as that visible on Nosegay (g).

The flat hand lamp (e) was illustrated in a New Martinsville Glass Co. catalogue,[1] and listed as No. 100. A lamp with a handle and base like (a), and a plain font like (b), was numbered 250.

Hanson (f) was illustrated with leaf and flower decoration on the fonts, bases and chimneys. It was available in ten variations of size and type, and was listed as: "No. 702 / LINE OF OPAL LAMPS / Cold Stain Decoration No. 31". The chimneys, with similar decoration on what appears to be a frosted band, were described as: "Sun Chimneys, Decoration / No.21 Burned-in".

This company, which started up in 1901 at New Martinsville WV, is still operating today as Viking Glass Co.[2] It is possible that some of these sequentially-related lamps may have been made by another factory who sold the molds to New Martinsville when they started up.

Hanson and Nosegay are also illustrated in OL I.

d. Stippled Fishscale and Rib

e. Nosegay flat hand

f. Hanson

g. Nosegay with ribbed base

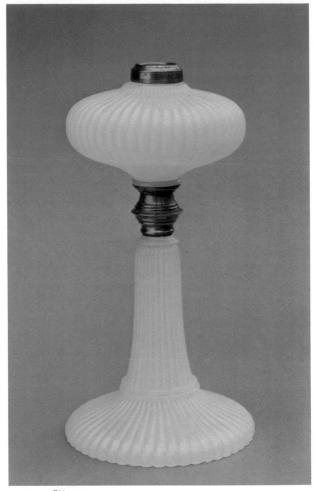

a. Illuminator. Clear font, opaque white base
b. Eaton.[ON] Opaque white font, blue alabaster base

c. Eaton.[ON] White alabaster

Undoubtedly made at Sandwich, and unmistakably illustrated in the Atterbury & Co. 1872 and 1874 catalogues,[1] the lamps commonly called Onion, (b), (c) and pictured on p. 17, are identified in the Atterbury price lists as Eaton lamps. They were made in blue, lavender or heliotrope, green and opaque white.

The abundance of lamp and match holder fragments found at Sandwich, and the superb quality of glass and design are the basis of attribution to Sandwich. Several members of an Eaton family were associated with the Sandwich company.[2]

The inclusion of these lamps in the Atterbury catalogues, poses some questions. Did they actually make any of the Eaton lamps; and if so were they colorless, colored, opaque or transluscent? Although much of the Atterbury glass was second rate mass production, examples extant exhibit first quality glass and workmanship. The Midwest could have been the origin of some of these lamps.

The connector on the Eaton lamps is a two-part threaded type. The top and bottom sections are cemented to the font and base pegs respectively. Atterbury made limited use of this connector.[3]

It is possible that future research will yield more information about the production of these lamps.

Sizes are: (a) 11-1/2'', (b) 13-1/2'', (c) 13-1/2'', (d) 11-1/2'', (e) 9-3/4'', (f) 9''.

Opposite ▷

Blue opalescent early composite lamp with appropriate chimney and burner, 1860's. Brass stem and marble base; collar replaced. Height 8''.

d. and e. Illuminators,[ON] all glass

f. Illuminator,[ON] iron base

Composite
Lamps

Composite kerosene lamps with glass fonts evolved from solar lamps with metal fonts; and from whale-oil or burning-fluid lamps with brass stems and marble bases. In the early 1860's, pressed-glass bases joined to the fonts with brass connectors, became popular. Later, in the 60's, cast iron was used with brass connectors and stems; or occasionally as a completely cast font holder that obviated the use of a brass connector.

The popularity of the separate pressed-glass bases in opaque white and colors diminished rapidly in the late 1870's. Cast-iron bases however became larger and more complex. They remained popular until the mid 1880's.

Figural stems of cast spelter, or occasionally brass or bronze, were used with gas fixtures and solar lamps. The first kerosene banquet lamps often had glass fonts mounted on these bases. Quality and design varied greatly until it reached what must be the ultimate in the example illustrated here — a composite figural lamp featuring a lady holding a composite lamp!

This lamp, those opposite and one on p. 86 are from a reprinted Edward Miller & Co. Illustrated Catalogue of Bronzed, Decorated and Real Bronze Lamps and Cigar Lighters, dated 1881. Located in Meriden, Connecticut, this company was also one of the largest manufacturers of kerosene burners. Most of the catalogue's 100 pages illustrate composite lamps. It is the most valuable primary source of information about composite kerosene lamps made after 1865. Included are brass stems shown in the Russell and Erwin 1865 catalogue, combined with cast-iron bases. Poets, putti and a princess, as well as a baseball player, scientist and cigar-smoking wench are featured among the figural lamps.

Also illustrated are many examples of composite lamps with glass stems that continued to be popular for more than two decades. For a few dollars the inexpensive models advertised in mail-order catalogues offered a semblance of grandeur to the farmhouse parlor.

Examples in this section range from the most commonplace to the most exceptional lamps made in America.

Catalogue illustrations courtesy of Fairweather Antiques, Meriden, Connecticut.

The finishes available for these lamps were listed as ''French Bronze, Light Verde, Dark Green, Electro Green, Electro Blue, Electro Plain & c.'' Although the glass was not described, it is evident from the illustrations and from examples extant, that the range included both lead and lime glass, that was often roughed or acid etched, engraved or cut. In addition there was painted, enamelled and gilded opaque glass.

a.

b.

c.

d.

e.

f.

g.

h.

i.

j.

k.

l.

The twenty-four lamps illustrated on these two pages, were photographed in several U.S. locations. Catalogues and price lists of the late 1850's and the 1860's indicate a substantial production of cased and cut lamps. This sampling, from private collections, antique shops and an auction house indicate a great variety has survived. A few of the font and base combinations may not be original.

The most common cased and cut lamps have white cut to clear or ruby fonts. Blue was also popular. Pink, amethyst and green are relatively scarce.

One of the most interesting aspects of cased and cut lamps is the manner in which the interior is viewed through the cut areas. Each concave area becomes a lens and the total effect depends upon the depth of the cutting and the design of the font. A single or inner layer of white glass shows this most clearly.

a. Several features of this lamp are unusual. Among them are the dramatic effect of the geometric cutting and the short double-step pressed base.

b. The design of this font has been called the "Washington Cut". It is seen in various proportions, sizes and colors.

c. Pear-shaped font with stylistic floral cutting.

d. White cut to ruby font with bold cutting that includes stars and quatrefoil. Opaque white Baroque base with gilding.

e. White cut to dark green. Two-part connector and white alabaster Baroque base with gilding.

f. White cut to ruby. The cut areas are relatively small. Opaque white patterned base.

g. White cut to blue font with the same design as *(e)*. White alabaster base.

h. The relatively large cut areas of this font create a light open feeling.

i. Little remains of the gilt pattern that once encircled this font.

j. The Boston & Sandwich Glass Company advertised two lamps with this stem and base design. Combined here with the rich gilt scroll design on the font, it makes an exceptional lamp.

k. Simplicity and proportion are the qualities that contribute to the success of this lamp.

l. A large area of this font was left uncut to accommodate the foliate gilt design. Baroque base.

m. Another "Washington Cut" font in amethyst cut to clear. The bronze finish fluted stem is mounted on a double step opaque white, pressed glass base.

n. Geometric cut font, green to clear. Opaque white Baroque base.

o. Opaque white cut to clear. Design includes rough-cut leaves. Black glass Baroque base.

p. Simple white cut to ruby design. Design patented base, made by the New England Glass Company, has gilt accents.

q. White cut to ruby font with a distinctive stylized vine design. The stem, used on 1847 Solar lamps,[1] was continued through the mid-1860's. (see p. 147 & 151)

r. Traces of a gilt design surround each of the large "windows". White cut to ruby. The metal parts have a bronze finish.

s. Red outer layer cut to white and clear. Worn gilt pattern on the font is the same as that on *(t)*. Bronze-finish metal parts include an unusual stem.

t. Deep pink cut to white and clear. The gilt scroll design is in excellent condition.

u. Tomato-red cut to white and clear in a bold geometric design.

v. The gold cartouche on the opaque white font would have originally framed a painted polychrome decoration. Style of base with cut stem was used in the 1850's for pre-kerosene lamps.

w. Pink cut to white and clear. This font has the same cutting as *(e)* and *(g)*. Blue alabaster base with worn gilt trim. A two-part connector was used.

x. White cut to ruby font with quatrefoil. Early fluted stem with brass or bronze mounts, characteristic of pre-kerosene lamps.

These lamps are typical of the styles made between the late 1850's and the early 1870's. Most, if not all, are from the East.

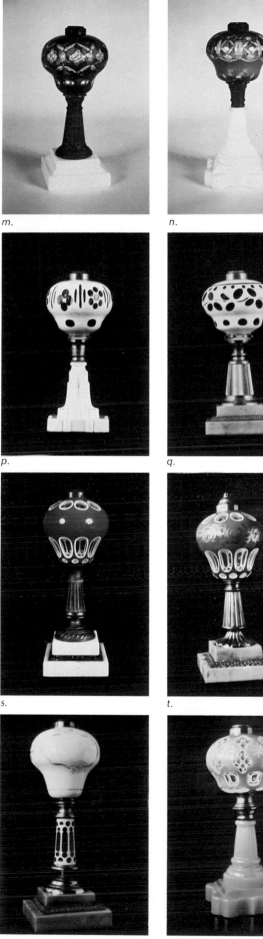

m. *n.* *o.*

p. *q.* *r.*

s. *t.* *u.*

v. *w.* *x.*

b. Air-trap band font

a. Cut glass Diamond and Oval Mitered Panels

Colorless, deeply cut glass lamps of the 1850's and 60's, are surprisingly rare today compared with examples of colored or cased and cut glass of the same period. The only other example the writer has seen is the one illustrated in the 1865 Russell and Erwin catalogue (see p. 151, No. 8591). On that example a much smaller area of the surface was cut.

a. This example has a bold design covering most of the font. Deeply cut mitered panels have alternate designs of ovals and diamonds. The slender spun-brass stem and double marble base with a cast-brass step contribute to a well-proportioned lamp.

b. During the 1815-1835 period, free-formed pieces of glass with tooled air-trap bands were made at two Boston companies managed by Thomas Cains. Included were many examples of lamps in styles that disappeared in the 1840's. Except for the air-trap band, the lamp above has all the characteristics of an 1860 lamp. This suggests a revival of this technique, possibly by Cains himself. It may be a unique example of this period.[1]

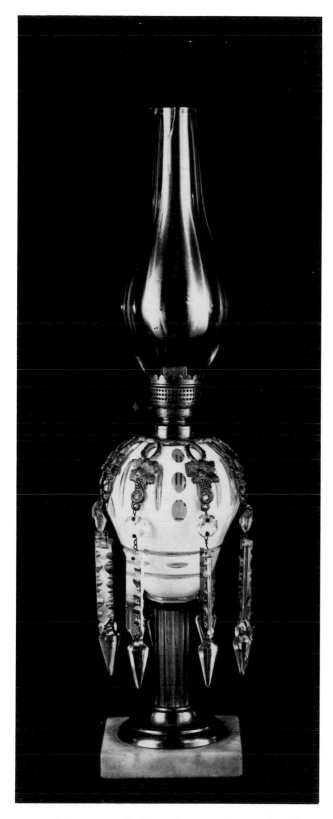

c. Partially concealed by a brass prism ring with cut glass prisms, is a deeply cut opaque white glass font with a crisp geometric design. Both this lamp and (d) are probably from the late 1850's or early 60's.

d. This large early bullseye font is mounted on a base made for a solar lamp. The stem, with Art Nouveau characteristics apparent in many decorative pieces of the 1850's, retains its original ormolu finish.

a. This banquet lamp is illustrated on plate 77 of the Boston and Sandwich Glass Co. catalogue circa 1865. Although it is listed as opal, another lamp with the same decoration on the same page is listed as alabaster. The prism ring and prisms, in keeping with the illustration, are a recent addition.

b. & c. It could be argued that the Divided Heart font is a replacement; however, the matching gilt green alabaster font is definitely original. The stems of these lamps and the lamp pictured in OL I p. 239 are illustrated in several colors and combinations in the Dietz catalogue, plates 1-3, along with the lamps of foreign manufacture. The possibility that the glass parts were imported should not be ruled out. It could account for the use of such a variety of bases and pre-kerosene connectors found on examples extant.

d. The illustration of this lamp on plate 77 of the *Boston & Sandwich Co.* catalogue, shows prisms hanging from a prism ring on the font and from another ring at the connector. Prisms were probably fastened to the leaves on this example. Although the *Russell and Erwin* catalogue (see p. 151) describes it as being available in assorted colors, I have seen it only in green and in blue cased with white.

e. This lamp is not illustrated in the *Boston & Sandwich Co.* catalogue, however the quality and the shape, similar to *(d)*, indicate it may have been made there. On the stem, the wider circles of the white casing are due to a thicker layer. This seems to be a common condition of these lamps.

f. The thick white casing emphasizes the excellent cutting on this lamp. Both the example *(e)* and this lamp effectively illustrate the lenses created by the concave cutting. The heavy brass connectors on these lamps have a definite flare that creates a distinctive identifiable profile in the *Boston & Sandwich Co.* catalogue pages. They are not apparent in the *Dietz* catalogue.

a.

b.

c.

d.

e.

f.

g.

h.

a. This well-detailed figural stem interjects a little humor into the lamp scene. The proportion of the little girl's wrists indicates a tomboy toughness in spite of her well-groomed appearance and prim costume. With obvious glee she holds back her cat with a firm grip on its tail, while dangling a mouse over her left knee. This might represent a fictional character, or perhaps a social comment.

The font has a brushed, frosted finish with cut circles and the base is slate, painted black. Height 10-3/8''.

b. The base of this lamp is called Madelaine in OL I, however Eve is probably more appropriate because the lady appears to be offering an apple. Identical illustrations of a lamp with this base and a font similar to (a), with a ball shade, are shown in OL I p. 107 on the reproduced Boston and Sandwich Co. catalogue page, as well as on plate 28 of the Dietz catalogue. Both are described as No. 33. 13-1/2 in. Dietz, on plate 36, also offered the base only, described as No. 26. 8 inch.

A number of these lozenge-shaped fonts are included along with others in a photograph of stock offered for sale by the Mt. Washington Glass Company.[1] In the absence of this evidence it might easily be assumed that the font was unique because it is so very different from other kerosene fonts. The distinctive shape, with deep rough-cut periphery, is an indication of the potential inherent in colorless glass when the designer and craftsman are not restrained by convention. Height 11-1/4''.

Cast-iron one-piece lamp bases would seem to be a very good solution for lamp bases however, relatively few are found today. The bases (c) to (h) appear to have preceded the common one or two part cast-iron bases that required a brass connector.

All fonts in the examples here are typical of those made in the 1860's. The round base (f) has the same vintage detail as a call bell patented in the 1850's and manufactured in West Meriden, CT by one of the largest lamp and burner manufacturers.

c. Wedding Ring. This mold-blown font is the only example I have seen of the more common excellent quality pressed design shown in OL I p. 166 e. Also illustrated in the Russell and Erwin catalogue, pp. 149-150.

d. Barred Rib Swirl. Mold-blown font similar to those found on small all-glass stand lamps of the 1860's.

e. Greek Key with Scalloped Band. Mold-blown font of fair quality, featuring popular design details of the 1860's.

f. Blown font with simple well-executed cut design. The distinctive broad pear shape is characteristic of many cased and cut fonts.

g. Pressed Icicle. This font, also shown on an opaque white base on p. 83 g, is an example of exceptional design and workmanship.

h. Quasi-Greek Key with Leaf. The deceptive geometric band is often thought to be the familiar Greek Key pattern at first glance. Another similar design is illustrated on p. 74 e.

i.

j.

Both the Boston and Sandwich catalogue and the Dietz company catalogue show lamps with these bases combined with fonts having the same roughed (on a lathe) surface and engraved design; but with different metal parts. Dietz also offered the bases separately, (see p. 88).

On *(j)* the original antique gold finish is almost perfect, however the quality of the cast spelter on *(i)* and *(j)* is only mediocre. Height: *(i)* 14-1/8'' and *(j)* 13-1/2''.

a. b. c. d. e. & f.

g.

h.

i.

j.

k.

l.

m.

The lamps on these pages include several rare examples of the glassmaker's art of the 1860's.

a. Blown ruby glass font combined with a square opaque pressed-glass base.

b. This transparent ruby glass font with slightly swirled loopings is a superior example of threaded glass.

c. The white canes below the cranberry casing appear to be light pink in this attractive example of latticinio glass.

d. Cranberry overshot or craquelle font with cut vertical stripes, accented by gilding.

e. Cased cranberry font with ground leaf, having a polished cut outline and accents.

f. Victorian flower holder. Similar ones in cast iron, with single or double arms, were manufactured in the 1880's by Bradley & Hubbard in Meriden, CT. They were advertised as ivy or flower holders, however today they are most often mistakenly labelled float lamps.[1]

g. A rare and unusual threaded cranberry font with a white outer casing, cut in an unusual paw-print design.

h. Pear-shaped font with spiralled white threads.

i. Latticinio font with blue and white threads, not completely marvered into the surface.

j. Globular font with spiralled white threads.

k. Six Blue Striper. This type of font was named by Preston R. Bassett, and attributed by him to the Joseph Walter & Co. Flint Glass Works, Williamsburgh, NY. Five Blue Striper fonts, the more common variety, were made in other shapes as well.[2]

l. Colorless font with pink and white loopings.

m. Pink loopings on an opaque white font.

n.

o.

p. q. r. & s.

The technique of dragging or looping threads of glass was practiced in both the East and Midwest. Examples in a variety of forms are among the most impressive pieces in collections of American Glass. See Innes pp.100-103.

n. The workmanship, color, glass quality and shape of this font combine to produce an object with apparent vitality. The prosaic base does not detract. Approx. 11''.

o. Both the shape and the bold pink and blue loopings give this font the appearance of strength. The monumental character of the base is appropriate.

p. Alabaster melon font; gold stripes. The pressed base, also gilded, has an uncommon shape. H. 9''.

q. Clear font with spiralled opaque white threads, combined with a pressed black base. Height 9-7/8''.

r. This rare lamp was even more spectacular when the original fine gilt tracery covered the entire cased area. The unusual base with white swirled stripes shading to blue was probably the result of canes of white glass dropped into the mold before black glass with predominantly blue colorants was introduced.

s. Another pear-shaped font with spiralled white threads. The prism ring and prisms are appropriate but not original. Height 12-1/8''.

t. Small opalescent, cased and cut to clear lamp. Height 7-1/2''.

u. Light amethyst blown font with excellent quality; fiery opalescent base. Height 8-1/2''.

v. Panelled Cloverleaf Crest in fiery opalescent glass. Also made were colorless all-glass lamps with this font. Height 8-1/4''.

w. White alabaster glass font; gold bands. H. 8''.

x. Reed and Plain Bands in opaque white.

y. Eyes and Diamonds. Mold-blown font with fiery opalescent base. Height 8-1/2''.

t.

u.

v.

w.

x.

y.

b. Engraved and cut Swag and Tassel design.

Courtesy Richard A. Bourne Co., Inc.

a. Ruby cased lamp cut to clear.

a. This lamp combines the cut design of a lamp illustrated in the Boston & Sandwich Glass Co. catalogue circa 1865, with the overall shape of others made by this company. Appropriate chimneys and shades for these lamps considerably enhance their appearance.

b. The delicate design of the engraving on this lamp circa 1860, follows the tradition of pre-kerosene whale-oil and burning-fluid lamps.

c. Onion Repeat. The onion design at the base of this pressed font is repeated in a modified form above the horizontal ring. This name was therefore too tempting to ignore. Height 10-1/2''.

d. Moon and Crescents. The exceptional calibre of the designer's, moldmaker's and glassmaker's skills are evident in this rare pressed font. Both lamps on this page are circa 1865. Height 12-1/2''.

a.

b.

c.

d.

e.

f.

g.

h.

i.

j.

k.

l.

There are pronounced variations in color and quality among the examples of cased and cut lamps illustrated here. All lamps of this type have generally been considered to be products of the East. Perhaps future research will reveal the Midwest as the source of some of these lamps. It is probable that all of these lamps were made in the 1860's or earlier. These cased and cut lamps and those in the balance of this section are described in the manner of the Boston & Sandwich catalogue, eg: cut blue over clear or cut blue over white and clear.

a. Poor quality glass was rarely used for cased and cut lamps. As with all glass, the imperfections can create a texture or interesting effect. In this example, shown also in OL I p. 164 a, the texture, due to tiny bubbles or *seeds*, adds to the character of this lamp with a rich amethyst casing over clear glass. Height 10-1/2''.

b. Cut amethyst over clear. A neat shape popular in the 1860's and perhaps late 1850's.

c. Cut medium to deep pink over white and clear. The base is a replacement.

d. Cut amethyst over white and clear with very good quality workmanship.

e. Cut cobalt blue over clear. This font, essentially the same as 56 *(e)* has the rough cut leaves in a lateral positon. The black glass base has worn gilding in a delicate design.

f. Cut opaque white over cobalt blue. It is evident the craftsman who produced this font was far off the mark. Light blue alabaster base with gilt bands.

g. Cut deep rose over white and clear with scrolled gilt decoration. Alabaster Baroque base.

h. Cut opaque white over ruby. White base with gilt bands.

i. Pear-shaped font in opaque white cut to green. Turquoise alabaster base.

j. Rough and polished cutting were used in this geometric design. Cut green over clear. The ormolu and black finish on the brass parts of the base is in exceptionally fine condition.

k. Excellent cutting is evident on this simple but unusual cut opaque white over clear font. It makes a striking lamp combined with the gilt decorated white base.

l. Washington cut, undoubtedly named after the well-known glass pattern. Cut ruby over clear on a stepped opaque white base with clean lines.

m.

n.

The Sandwich *tours de force!* These immense cut blue and white over clear lamps are illustrated with minor variations, on plate 77 of the Boston & Sandwich Glass Co. catalogue, circa 1865. (see OL I p. 107). The one on the left is described as "Cut Punty and Diamond Flint"; and the one on the right as "Cut Opal over Flint." The lamps in the catalogue are shown with cut glass shades that do not match the design of the lamps. Heights: *(m)* 28" and *(n)* 28-1/2". Weight: over 23 pounds each!

a. Waffle and Thumbprint

b. Block on Block

c. Diamond Band and Ribs

d. Diamond Band and Cable

e. Ellipse Band and Rib

All lamps on these two pages were made in the 1860's.

a. Waffle and Thumbprint, height 10-1/8". The wide flat base on an otherwise globular font is an indication that the design was also used for lamps with nearly cylindrical fonts, usually associated with whale oil or burning fluid. One of these in the Waffle and Thumbprint pattern is illustrated in Kenneth M. Wilson's, *New England Glass and Glassmaking*, (fig. 249). Also illustrated, (fig. 290), is a page from an 1868 New England Glass Company Catalogue showing two goblets in the Waffle and Thumbprint pattern.

b. Block on Block is an interesting design well-suited to a pressed font. It is the only example the writer has seen. Approx. 10".

c. Diamond Band and Ribs. The design of this mold-blown font is reminiscent of earlier American glass patterns.

d. Diamond Band and Cable. This busy pressed pattern combines simple geometric shapes with a cable design. Approx. 8-1/2".

e. Ellipse Band and Rib. This font should be compared with (a) and (b) on p. 82. Although similar, this one does not have the plain panels or round protrusion at the base. Instead the vertical portion has pronounced ribs. Approx. 8".

f. Diamond Band and Fan

g. Shell Panel

h. M'Kee Shell

f. Diamond Band and Fan. Shown in OL I p. 102 in a mold-blown flat hand lamp with applied handle and distinct diamonds. The pressed font shown here was over-expanded and has distorted diamonds.

In addition, the ill-proportioned No. 1 collar detracts from the lamp. See p. 149 for the illustration of this lamp in the Russell and Erwin catalogue pages. It is also shown in the Dietz catalogue on plates 8 and 34.

Five smaller fonts in this pattern, mounted in an ornate set of girandoles, were displayed in a shop in Georgia. They all had whale-oil burners that appeared to be original. Approx. 11''.

g. Shell Panel is a pressed pattern with good definition and excellent quality glass. Height 11-3/4''.

h. M'Kee Shell appears to be the one illustrated in the 1864 and 1868 catalogue, (see p. 31). Some of the drawings are rather difficult to interpret; however in the example here, the pointed detail at the base between the shells and the shape and juxtaposition of the shells appear to be as illustrated. Height 9-1/2''.

i. Shell and Dart, a mold-blown pattern is illustrated in two sizes and on two different bases in the Russell and Erwin catalogue, (see p. 149). It is also illustrated in the Dietz catalogue. Height 7-7/8''.

j. Inverted Leaf Panel is a mold-blown pattern that could have been easily adapted to a flat hand lamp with the entire font inverted. Height 8-1/2''.

i. Shell and Dart

j. Inverted Leaf Panel

a.

b.

c.

d.

e.

f.

Red, white and blue lamps are featured on these pages. The shades, typical of those illustrated in the 1860's catalogues are all replacements.

a. Cut opaque white over blue alabaster. This lamp and shade closely resemble No. 962 on plate 11 of the Dietz catalogue.

b. Elegant cut blue over clear. Both font and shade of this beautifully-proportioned lamp have rough and polished cut surfaces.

c. Cut ruby over clear shade and font. Polished and rough cut stylized floral design. Opalescent No. 40 base.

d. Cut blue over clear font with gilt decoration in superb condition. Lighter blue alabaster base with gilt bands.

e. Cut opaque white over ruby. A lively popular design, illustrated in the Dietz catalogue.

f. Cut dark blue over clear. The geometric design and cutting on this font have resulted in an unusual optical effect.

g. Cut ruby over clear. Geometric design on a relatively large font.

h. Cut blue over opaque white and clear. This design was also made with a pink outer layer. The extremely thin middle layer has resulted in a very fine white outline around the cut areas.

i. Cut ruby over clear. This is a modified version of the design on font (c).

g.

h.

i.

The hundreds of colored lamps offered for sale in catalogues of the late 1850's and 1860's and the variety extant, establishes the fact that the first decade of kerosene lamps represents an astonishing record of outstanding American glassmaking.

j. Cut ruby over clear. Base and font combinations often resulted in ill-proportioned lamps. The substantial wide base serves to balance the proportion of the large font.

k. Cut ruby over clear lamp and shade. This magnificient example is essentially the same as lamps illustrated in the Boston & Sandwich Glass Co. catalogue. The glass and cutting are as close to perfection as can be found on any lamp of this type. Stems, because they are not expanded as much as the fonts, generally have a thicker casing resulting in a deeper color. Circa 1865. Height to top of the collar 16''.

j. Stand lamp circa 1865

Photograph courtesy of the Royal Ontario Museum

k. Banquet lamp, probably by the Boston & Sandwich Glass Co.

a. Gothic

Most of the patterns on these two pages were also made in tableware pieces. The addition of a few matching goblets or pieces of other glassware broadens the scope of a lamp collection.

a. A lamp is not included in the 16 pieces of the Gothic pattern listed by Ruth Webb Lee.[1] The soft pattern definition and brilliant glass combine to produce an almost fluid appearance, compared to the crisp lines usually associated with this type of pressed font. (See also p. 151).

b. Stedman. The reprinted M'Kee and Brothers catalogues provide a good deal of information about this pattern,[2] (see p. 31).

It first appeared in an undated price list judged to have been issued in the 1863-64 period. Stedman composite and all-glass footed lamps were listed. An assortment described as ''pressed assorted large pegs'', also included Stedman. This is rather puzzling, because the Stedman font (b) is mold-blown, although the M'Kee Tulip lamp fonts are pressed. Height: 8-7/8''.

The 1864 and 1868 catalogues list the same variety of Stedman lamps; and illustrate the stand lamps.

c. Beaded Mirror. This pattern is attributed to the Boston Silver Glass Company. Circa 1870.[3] The definition and quality of this pressed font are excellent. The base is not the original one; however it is appropriate. Height: 9''.

d. Lincoln Drape. This graceful pressed pattern is well suited to a lamp font. Matching pieces should be easier to locate than the lamp.

e. Washington. This pattern was illustrated in the New England Glass Company catalogue circa 1870.[4] The font, and the black double marble base with brass step having an ormolu and black finish, however, appear to have been made earlier, in the 1860's. Height: 10-7/8''.

f. Periwinkle. This pattern differs too much from the M'Kee vine pattern to attribute it to that company. Periwinkle, a common name for Vinca, a creeping ground-cover, is a name others have used. An example in a more conventional shape is shown on p. 110.

g. Acorn. This is another pressed pattern with a fine ribbed background. Circa 1860's or possibly earlier. Height: 9''.

b. Stedman

c. Beaded Mirror

d. Lincoln Drape

e. Washington

f. Periwinkle

g. Acorn

a.

b.

d.

e.

f.

c.

a. Cut blue font over white and clear. Chartreuse base 4-1/2'' square. Height: 9-11/16''.

b. Pressed honeycomb font in canary. Pressed black glass base.

c. Ring Punty Sawtooth and Eye. Two other examples of this popular 1860's pattern are illustrated in OL I p. 86. The canary base, rarely seen on kerosene lamps, was often used for vases and candlesticks.

d. Double Semi-circles. Medium green alabaster blown font that was also made in a very dark green. Opaque white pressed base.

e. Mold-blown font and pressed base in green alabaster glass. Worn gilt decoration includes bands and Greek Key motif.

f. Bullseye Panel pressed font in colorless glass. Pressed dark green base.

g. Teal blue blown font. This is another color more often seen in the form of candlesticks or vases. The pressed glass base is an unusual design.

h. Filley font in transparent blue glass. This font and the Gem base suggest this may have been an Atterbury & Co. lamp of the mid-1860's.

i. Blue alabaster font with painted floral decoration.

All of the lamps on this page are typical of the late 1850's and 1860's.

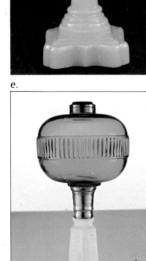

g.

h.

i.

j.

j. A delicately engraved and stained presentation lamp, with four stained and engraved medallions, (two floral, one landscape with deer and one R.F. Fish/1860). If such gifts had been more popular and cherished, the history of glassmaking in America would have been much easier to record but considerably less challenging.

This particular lamp is attributed to the Boston & Sandwich Glass Co., Sandwich, MA, circa 1860. Fish was one of the better-known names associated with the Boston & Sandwich Glass Co. Local records reveal many residents with the surname Fish; however, the recipient of this example has not been positively identified.[1] Height: 8''.

k. & l.

k. Green alabaster font and base. Relatively few mold-blown fonts had patterns at the upper portion of the font. Most patterns covered only the lower half to two-thirds of the area, following the general appearance of pressed fonts like (l). The brass collar and connector differ in appearance from other lamps of this type. This could mean they were from a manufacturer with relatively small production, or there is always the possibility that the lamp was imported.

l. Four Petal Band. The general character and proportion of this design is similar to the Four Petal pattern shown in OL I p. 112. The green Baroque alabaster base was an admirable choice. Beside these lamps is a wick trimmer, used to take care of a routine chore associated with kerosene lighting.

a. Sunken Circles

b. Crossed Cannons

c. Stars and Eyes

d. Ringed Bullseye Band

e. Stars Entwined

All of the lamps on these two pages, except (c) were mold-blown. The basic shapes and patterns vary considerably.

a. Sunken Circles. A small 1860's lamp with pleasing proportion. An example of this font in opaque blue, combined with a square pressed base is shown in *Heritage of Light* by Loris S. Russell.[1]

b. Crossed Cannons. Hunting horns alternate with cannons on the font of this 1860's lamp. It is an unusual departure from the more common floral and geometric patterns.

c. Stars and Eyes. Pressed font with good quality glass. Height: 8-7/8''.

d. Ringed Bullseye Band. Mid-1860's font with simple geometric design. Height: 7-7/8''.

e. Stars Entwined. The post-1876 replacement collar is evident on this lamp. All other characteristics, and the Russell and Erwin illustration p. 148, point to an 1860's date. Height: 7-7/8''.

f. Bow and Rib

g. Melon

h. Tapered Rib

f. Bow and Rib. The design of this font closely resembles pressed patterns of the 1860's. Height: 10".

g. Melon. A good quality font. This simple design was probably made by several companies.

h. Tapered Rib. A matching hand lamp with font reversed is shown on p. 98d. Height: 7-1/2".

i. Inverted Leaf and Chevron. Both the post-1876 collar and the shape of this font, suggest an 1870's date. The base may have been a leftover from earlier days.

j. Broad Melon. Six well-defined segments make this one of the most distinctive simple fonts of the 1860's.

i. Inverted Leaf and Chevron

j. Broad Melon

a.

b.

c.

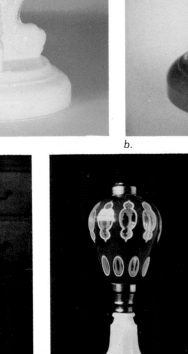

d.

e.

f.

Triple Dolphin lamps are among the most important lamps widely acknowledged to have been made by the Boston & Sandwich Glass Co. Only about four of the over 75 pages of their 1860's catalogue have been found leaving the possibility that Triple Dolphin lamps could have been advertised on another page, or they could have made them before or after the catalogue was printed.

Bases were made in black, white and colors. All I have examined were from the same mold. The most obvious characteristic is the mold seam on one of the dolphins located well to the right of centre as it passes over the head.

a. A fiery opalescent base combined with a pressed Ring Punty, Sawtooth, Eye and Leaf font, (see OL I p. 86). Four of these fonts, in two sizes, have been seen on Triple Dolphin bases.

b. Opaque lavender base with Diamond and Loop Panel font, (see OL I p. 168 b). The font reflects the overhead lights in the arena where it was photographed.

c. A rare alabaster base with three dolphins. Cut opaque white over pink font. The quality is superb! The origin however is questionable. I suspect all or at least the base, was imported. Fonts of this design, familiar in America, could also have been imported.

d. to i. and (j) opposite. Moorish Windows seems to be an appropriate name for this cut design; perhaps the most common one of the 1860's judging by catalogues and examples extant.

Bases (d) to (i) include designs made from the 1850's to the early 1870's.

Opposite ▷

j. The Triple Dolphin lamp opposite is a fine example with matching yellow-green font and base.

g.

h.

i.

a. Ring, Scallops and Dart

b. Punctuated Loop

c. Bullseye Loop

All lamps on this page have pressed fonts and all of those opposite are mold-blown, with pressed glass bases. Pressed fonts, with a few exceptions such as the Dillaway lamps, do not have a pattern close to the shoulder, nor mold marks in that area. The glass is generally thicker, and better quality.

a. Ring, Scallops and Dart. An interesting pattern that continues through the pronounced ring around the middle. Height: 8-1/8''.

b. Punctuated Loop. Also illustrated in the Russell and Erwin catalogue (see p. 149) combined with a base similar to that of (a). It is certainly one of the most distinctive simple patterns on that catalogue page.

c. Bullseye Swirl. Scrolled designs suggest motion and this one is particularly successful in that respect, as well as in its general appearance.

d. Stars in Cubes. A large font, very good quality glass. Height: 11-1/2''.

e. Quasi-Greek Key and Swag. The design of this font is similar to the one on p. 54 h. Height: 11-5/8''.

These lamps would all have been made in the 1860's.

d. Stars in Cubes

e. Quasi-Greek Key and Swag

f. Grant^ON or Rand Rib

g. Birch Leaf

h. Star Brooch

f. Grant^ON or Rand Rib. Matching font and base in white alabaster. Relatively few early composite lamps have matching glass used for the font and base.

g. Birch Leaf. White alabaster font. This is a well-known pattern made in tableware and goblets. The stippling on the leaf is more apparent on colorless glass examples (see OL I p. 173). Opaque white Baroque base. Height: 8-1/4''.

h. Star Brooch. Fair to good quality glass and molding. Square pressed glass base. Approximtely 8''.

i. Star Pendants. Good quality glass, black Baroque base.

j. Melon with Fine Rib. See p. 102 c for hand lamp in this pattern and p. 110 d for an all-glass stand lamp. Not only is the pattern pleasing but it serves to conceal a flaw. The mold was either imperfect or slightly open causing what appears to be two mold seams, about 1/8'' apart. Height: 8-1/4''.

i. Star Pendants

j. Melon with Fine Rib

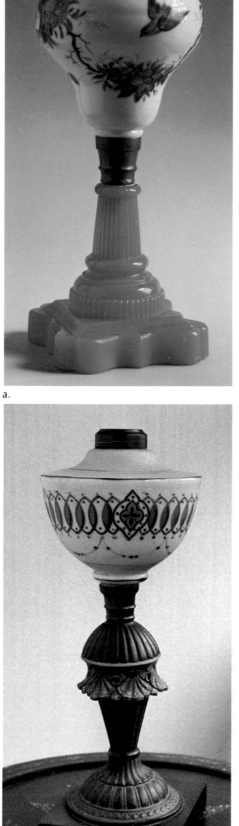

a.

b.

c.

d.

e.

Painted and enamelled lamps of the 1860's and 1870's are much less plentiful than examples of cased and cut lamps.

All of the lamps on this page have opaque white fonts with a cream or beige background color.

a. This rare font is painted in the manner of the decorated slant shades illustrated in a Boston & Sandwich Glass Co. catalogue of the 1870's. Combined with the blue alabaster Baroque base it is an outstanding lamp.

b. A rather elaborate setting is provided for the little bluebird on this font. A similar lamp is in the Chrysler Museum in Norfolk, VA.

c. Variations of this entwined ribbon have been seen on other fonts, including the one in OL I p. 111 d. Here it is combined with a medallion of flowers. Gilt bands and accents complete the decoration.

d. & e. The same design has been adapted to fonts with different shapes. The shape of (d) is similar to (f) on the opposite page, and (e) is a common pear shape. Gilt accents with Halloween colors of orange and black are surprisingly successful here.

f.

g.

h.

f. Painted, enamelled and gilded floral decoration on a pink alabaster font with satin finish. A similar font is illustrated in OL I p. 153 d. Another white font, similarly decorated, has been seen on a different figural base.

g. Green alabaster font and base. There is a similarity between the detailed veins and the gilt enamelled outline of the leaves on this font and font *(i)*.

h. Cut opaque white over clear. Abundant floral painted decoration, outlining, gilding and staining have been applied to this font. Combined with the decorated opaque white base it becomes a busy but colorful and interesting lamp.

i. The Wolf Stem lamp. Illustrated in the Boston & Sandwich and Dietz company catalogues, as well as in OL I p. 114 a. The polychrome finish on this spelter base could be original or possibly the work of a previous owner. It is incongruous with the fine opaque white font that has been painted, enamelled, gilded and accented with ruby glass "jewels".

j. This opaque white font has applied ruby "jewels" with painted, enamelled and gilded circles and festoons. It is combined with a green alabaster stem and double marble base. If lamps could talk this one would probably say "Merry Christmas."

i.

j.

a. Bullseye and Comma

b. Thumbprint and Feather Band

c. Whirling Wheels

d. Flute with Rib Fringe

e. Clip and Dart

f. Prisms and Diamond Point

a. Bullseye and Comma. Brilliant glass and excellent molding add to the success of this complex pattern. Square pressed opaque white base. Height: 10-1/4''.

b. Thumbprint and Feather Band. The design on this pressed font is essentially the same as that on the mold-blown example illustrated in OL I pp. 140-141. There is a difference in the direction and design of the feather band, but the two lamps are too simmilar to have different names. Opaque white pressed base.

c. Whirling Wheels. An interesting pattern that is similar to, but not the same as tableware patterns of the 1860's. This brilliant pressed glass font has a simple engraved design seen on many other fonts. The patented base was not original and was eliminated here to avoid confusion.

d. Flute with Rib Fringe. Like (c) above this font was obviously not part of an original combination. It is mold-blown with good definition.

e. Clip and Dart. Another pattern similar to 1860's tableware patterns. The brass connector on this lamp and on (f) are obvious and inappropriate replacements. Opaque white Baroque base. Height: 10-1/4''.

f. Prisms and Diamond Point. A fine quality pressed font. Lamps in this pattern were made in the pre-kerosene cylindrical form. This font has the characteristic base of the earlier lamps. Fair and sometimes poor quality mold-blown fonts with this design are much more common. Opaque white Baroque base. Height: 9-3/8''.

g. Triple Scallop and Rib Swag

h. Chadwick

i. Chadwick

g. Triple Scallop and Rib Swag. A different example of this font is shown in OL I p. 170 a combined with a replacement base. See p. 84 b for a similar example. Height: 12-1/8".

h. Chadwick. This pattern differs only slightly from Chapman, a pattern made and named by Atterbury & Co. In Chapman, there is a row of small diamonds above the pattern, and the ribbed ribbon portion has bars at right angles to the flow of the pattern (see p. 25 o). The juxtaposition of mold-blown and pressed fonts with the same pattern illustrates the characteristics of each technique.

i. Chadwick. Pressed example of the same pattern as *(h)*. Opaque white pressed base.

j. & k. Star and Loop Panel. These brilliant pressed fonts are two different sizes. The simple design engraved on the shoulder of the fonts is the same. Both pressed bases are opaque white.

These bases indicate the remarkable number of Baroque base variations that were made in the 1860's. The lamps on these two pages are from the 1860's or early 1870's.

j. Star and Loop Panel

k. Star and Loop Panel

a. Lamp with Bennington flint enamel base. Blue, grey and yellow balluster stem; grey, green and yellow double step base with 1849 mark impressed on the bottom.[1] Clear blown, cut and engraved pear-shaped font, decorated with cut lyre, and engraved leaf and vine. See p. 151 and OL I p. 108 c for other examples. Height: 16-3/16''.

b. A lamp with verve! Cut orange-red over opaque white and clear font with applied peg. The bold design, executed with more personality than perfection, is enhanced by the unusual bright color. This font was an excellent choice for the lively cast-spelter figure stem; mounted on a soapstone base, painted black. Height: 18-3/4''.

c.

d.

c. Cut orange-red over clear font. Collar marked "PAT AUG 27 67 JUN 17 68". Fluted brass stem and double marble base.

d. Cut ruby over clear. Design on the broad pear-shaped font includes panels with deeply cut icicle pattern. Brass stem and double marble base.

e. Cut opaque white over transparent pink. Another example is illustrated on p. 64 e. This font is also illustrated in the Dietz catalogue. The colorful Spatter Ware base is a rare example.

f. Crackle font. Ruby over clear and white on a black base. This lamp is considered by the Sandwich Museum to have been an experimental type manufactured by the Cape Cod Glass Company in Sandwich, MA. Their attribution was determined by comparison with a similar piece of well-documented glass. Height: 11-3/4".

g. Cut tomato-red over opaque white and clear. The wide outline of the vintage design is due to the angle of the cutting and the thick layer of opaque white glass.

g.

a. Diamond Band and Fine Rib

b. Ellipse Band and Fine Rib

c. Diamond and Scroll

d. Shields with Star Band

e. Leaf Panel

a. & b. Diamond Band and Fine Rib; and Ellipse Band and Fine Rib are almost identical designs. The Diamond Band font is a good quality mold-blown font. However, the quality of the glass used for the Ellipse Band font is poor but interesting. Numerous bubbles or *seeds,* some of which have broken on the surface have given it a rough texture. Approx. 9'' high.

c. Diamond and Scroll. Although the most prominent design motif on this lamp is the same as on the flat hand lamp p. 98 l, each has an entirely different pattern at the sides. The flat hand lamp also has a distinctive shape.

The pattern above with wide lines, has been roughed on a lathe. The base, like that shown on p. 26 d, is painted orange. I have seen another example in green and one with the lower step and stem in mauve with gilt bands. H: 10-1/4''.

d. Shields with Star Band. I believe this would generally be considered to be the best designed of the many fonts with a shield motif. The fine quality, fiery opalescent base, is appropriate. Height: 8-7/8''.

e. Leaf Panel. This lamp is one of a pair made from the same mold. Mold-blown font with opaque white Baroque base.

f. Racquets

g. Pressed Icicle

h. Aster Band

f. Racquets. Pressed pattern, probably of the late 1860's or early 1870's. Opaque white Baroque base.

g. Pressed Icicle. Another example of this superb font is shown on p. 54 g. It must have required extraordinary skills to produce this large spherical font with an absence of mold marks and good definition of pattern at the base.

h. Aster Band. Excellent quality pressed font. This pattern was also made in a small hand-lamp form with an applied handle. Pressed opaque white Gem^ON base.

i. Eyes and Diamonds. Mold-blown font with geometric pattern. Opaque white pressed base. Height: 8-5/8''.

j. Scalloped Diamond Band and Wheel. Good quality distinctive pressed pattern. Opaque white pressed base. Height: 9-1/2''.

i. Eyes and Diamonds

j. Scalloped Diamond Band and Wheel

a.

b.

d.

e.

f.

g.

Blue and lavender glass is featured on these two pages. With the main emphasis on fonts, the great variety of colored bases is often overlooked.

a. Bullseye Swirl is shown in (g) below, and on p. 74 c. The unmarked No. 40 lavender base is semi-opaque with opalescence.

b. Triple Swag and Diamond. With the exception of the diamonds, this pattern is almost identical to Triple Swag and Bar, p. 79 g. The lavender-blue Baroque base is slightly shaded.

c. Grant[ON]. White alabaster mold-blown font. No. 40 translucent base with darker blue streaks.

d. Triple Diamond Medallion. This pattern appears to be an earlier version of the pattern called Washington, that was produced for the 1876 Centennial. Illustrations of this lamp in the Russell and Erwin catalogue, pp. 149-150 and in the Dietz catalogue circa 1865, confirm the earlier date. Opaque medium blue, slightly marbled, Baroque base with space between the "teeth" on the dentate band.

e. Mollard. This pattern includes short ribs on the shoulder of the font, ribs separating plain panels and an icicle ribbed design at the base. The medium blue alabaster base originally had a gilt leaf design on the corners. Height: 8''.

f. This font, typical of the early 1870's, may not be original. Opaque blue base with an unusual ribbed stem.

g. Bullseye Swirl. Pressed font with a slightly different shape from example (a) above. Like (f) this blue base is another example of an unusual design. Height: 9-3/4''.

h.

i.

j.

h. & i. Fonts (h) and (i) in blue and white alabaster, were undoubtedly made by the same glassmaker or factory. The example (h), with the additional ring below the shoulder of the font, appears to have a good finish. The rough texture of (i) is an indication of the deterioration commonly seen on alabaster glass of the 1850's. The style of bases further support an 1850's date.

j. Overshot or Craquelle font in a very pale blue. This round font is divided into segments by gilded and cut lines. Hexagonal black pressed base. This lamp circa 1860, is 9'' high.

k. & l. These lamp bases, in different shades of opaque blue, are similar to, but not exactly the same as bases made by Hobbs, Brockunier & Co., Wheeling, WV and illustrated in OL I pp. 151-154.

Font (k) is clear glass with frosted areas, ruby stain and gilding. The staining and condition of font (l) is excellent. Heights are: (k) 13-1/2'', (l) 12-3/8''. Circa 1870.

m. Bullseye Panel. Excellent pressed font of the 1860's. Opaque blue shaded base. Other examples of this base, in often poor quality opaque white, are illustrated in the Related Lamps section and in OL I p. 164 e. These bases are readily distinguished by their square corners.

n. Clear, frosted and stained font, with worn gilding. This rare, round shaded blue base, has a design similar to Leaf and Jewel, p. 122 d.

k.

l.

m.

n.

The tableware pattern, Star Band,[1] was evidently one of the most popular lamp patterns. The Star Band lamps shown in (fig. 1), from the Edward Miller & Co. 1881 catalogue and (a) below have different bases. The Henry & Nathan Russell & Day 1889 catalogue illustrates this font combined with a different Edward Miller base.[2]

Courtesy Fairweather Antiques.

fig. 1 Edward Miller & Co. ''No. 179-1/2 Lamp''

(a) Star Band on Edward Miller base

b. Miller No. 107 base

c. Bradley & Hubbard No. 030

d. Statue of Liberty Base

b. Miller No. 107 base. This is essentially the same base as illustrated in the 1881 Edward Miller & Co. catalogue. The cast-spelter base has been re-painted with gold paint. The panelled font with frosted finish has a simple cut design. Height: 11-5/8".

c. Bradley & Hubbard No. 030 base. This lamp was illustrated in a Bradley & Hubbard, West Meriden, CT catalogue. It is undated but appears to be from the 1870's. The font has clear panels framed by frosted areas. Each panel has a simple cut and engraved design. Height: 9".

d. Statue of Liberty base. This cast-spelter base closely resembles bottles that were made, probably during the same period. Other examples of almost identical patterns in cast spelter and blown glass have been seen. Circa 1880. The font is relatively small, but probably adequate for something that may have been marketed primarily as a souvenir.

e. Loop and Leaf with Beaded Band. Several examples of this mold-blown font have been seen.

f. Lyre and Scroll. Mold-blown pattern with fine lines. Similar in many respects to Panelled Shield OL I p. 103 i. This type of font would lend itself to being roughed on a lathe and some examples may be found finished this way.

e. Loop and Leaf with Beaded Band

f. Lyre and Scroll

a.

b.

c.

d.

e.

The composite lamps on these two pages include examples from the late 1850's to the mid-1890's.

a. Cut opaque white over ruby, broad pear-shaped font. The cut areas are relatively small. The base is illustrated and described on p. 55.

b. Three Graces. This cast-spelter figural stem, obviously made for a solar lamp, supports a free-blown pear-shaped opaque blue font. Late 1850's.

c. This base, also typical of the 1850's, has the air-intake holes near the connector that indicate its original intended use as part of a solar lamp. Cut blue over clear with rough and polished surfaces.

d. The Circus Bear. This delightful figural stem must have been very popular with children. The roughed and cut font is protected by the wide brass shoulder and base.

e. Sobering Up would be an appropriate name for this figural stem. The font, Notched Bullseye, is illustrated on a different base in OL I p. 167 h. Circa 1870.

f.

g.

h.

f. Roughed clear font with cut ovals. The cast-spelter stem, with excellent original finish, is in the form of a hand holding a pine cone. At the base of the hand is an elaborate folded cuff. Slate base painted black.

g. Optic Spatter font with Detroit Base. This composite lamp of the 1890's was made with unusual types of glass. The optic molded, swirled spatter font in this example, looks rather like a blue snowstorm. A similar example has been seen in light green, and a lamp with optic molded dots and very different coloration, is shown in OL I p 310 a.

h. Thousand Eye Variant. This lamp, circa 1890, is a more massive version of (j) below. Like the lamp below the font pattern is different from that of the base.

i. Juno. Another example of this purple marble or slag glass base is illustrated in OL I p. 216. It is a type of glass that was made in the Midwest by different companies around 1900. This example closely resembles glass made by Challinor, Taylor & Co., Tarentum, PA. The stained and engraved font differs from the one in OL I.

j. Thousand Eye with Diamond and Dot Font. Made by Adams & Company, this lamp was advertised in 1885 by Henry & Nathan Russell, New York manufacturers and distributors of lamps. This lamp, with a matching Thousand Eye font, is shown in OL I p. 262.

i.

j.

a. The Miller No. 1161 lamp. This lamp is identical to the one illustrated in the 1881 Edward Miller & Co. catalogue. Most of the cast-iron bases were comprised of several parts, which were often used in different combinations to increase the variety of designs offered. Mold-blown font with roughed finish.

b. Expanded Prism. This lamp, with a threaded screw connector or socket, was illustrated in the United States Glass Company catalogue circa 1893.

Opposite ▷

St. Louis in opaque white. This is one of three lamps named after U.S. cities and offered in the same catalogue.

a. & b.

c.

d.

e.

f.

g.

h.

i.

j.

k.

Catalogue illustrations courtesy Henry Ford Museum, The Edison Institute

A wide selection of colored composite lamps of the 1880's and 90's is illustrated here. Cathedral lamps, shown in OL I pp. 236-237, are known to have been made in various combinations of blue, amber and colorless glass. The interesting pair *(a)* & *(b)* shown here, have fluted Daisy and Button shades that were commonly used with different types of oil lamps. They appear to have been an original choice for these lamps circa 1890.

c. to k. These lamps are from hand-colored glossy catalogue pages printed on an oilcloth-type backing. The pink lamp *(g)*, is the Elite Princess, shown in a Consolidated Lamp and Brass Co. 1894 advertisement in Kamm VI. The lamp has a fancy lace shade instead of

the glass ball shade pictured here. There it is described as being available in rose, canary and turquoise glass, one color more than is offered here. It is difficult to determine if this catalogue was produced before or after the 1894 advertisement. The 1902 Consolidated Lamp and Brass Co. catalogue, advertising similar lamps, did not include any of the examples shown here. Many of these lamps were given a number for the style and color of decoration. Lamps *(c)*, *(d)*, and *(e)* are called the New Princeton Banquet Lamps. Waldo is the name of *(f)*, and *(g)* as mentioned, is Elite Princess. Lamp *(h)* is Olive Princess and the name given to *(l)*, written in ink below the lamp, cannot be deciphered. Myrtle is *(j)* and the tall cased pink lamp *(k)* is called Monastic.

l.

m. & n.

o. & p.

Glass was the most common material used for the stems of composite lamps with iron or slate bases that were popular between 1880 and early 1900. Fonts in a great variety of patterns were usually of colorless glass. Many were roughed on a lathe, a technique described on pp. 12-13, that can be readily identified upon close examination. Two-part Illuminator shades were appropriate with these lamps.

l. Bowtie Band. This popular font of the 1880's, is combined here with a redware stem with white glaze, decorated with blue flowers. Cast-iron stepped base.

m. Anthemion font with roughed finish. Attractive redware stem with predominantly blue glaze.

n. The Waffle design on this font resembles patterned chimneys of the 1880's. Redware stem with attractive farm scene.

o. Blue Hobnail font, possibly by Central Glass Company, Wheeling, WV. Circa 1885.

p. Blue Webster font shown also in OL I p. 177. Decorated opaque white glass stem.

q. Roughed patterned font with clear glass stem. Stems of this type (q), (r), (s) and (t), were inexpensively decorated on the inside with transfers and paint.

r. The pattern on this font is known as Frosted Circle, however in this example the circles are not frosted.

s. & t. Both are illustrated in the 1884 Henry & Nathan Russell Catalogue.

u. & v. These lamps, with different patterned fonts, have identical bases in different colors with enamelled floral designs.

w. Zig-Zag and Diamond font combined with an opaque white decorated glass stem.

x. This patterned font, with roughed surface, is combined with a redware stem in the form of a tree trunk.

q. & r.

s. & t.

u. & v.

w. & x.

No. 21 Princess Lamp
Complete Height 20 inches

Diana Princess
Lamp Complete. Height 21 inches

Colonial Princess
Lamp Complete. Height 20 inches

No. 2 Banquet Lamp
Height 18 inches

No. 17 Banquet Lamp
Height 19 in.

No. 1 Banquet Lamp
Height 25 inches

No. 4 Banquet Lamp
Height 25 inches

No. 25 Banquet Lamp
Height 19 inches

No. 25½ Banquet Lamp, Etched
Height 19 inches

Courtesy Fostoria Glass Company, Moundsville, WV.

Between 1900 and 1920 distinctive banquet lamps and candelabra were made by the Fostoria Glass Company, Fostoria, OH and the A.H. Heisey & Co. Newark, OH. In sharp contrast to cut-glass lamps, their uncluttered and sometimes severe design, may have been inspired by the same philosophy as the contemporary Mission furniture; or perhaps they were made to complement this radical new look.

Fostoria's designs, less restrained than those of Heisey, included lamps remarkably similar to the Baccarat lamps illustrated on p. 142.

WEDDING GIFTS

Dorflinger's American Cut Glass. 915 Broadway, New York

Courtesy, Henry Ford Museum, The Edison Institute

The extraordinarily large, elaborate and expensive kerosene lamps made between 1890 and 1915 are proof that there was still a market among the wealthy, long after the introduction of the electric light in the 1880's. Kerosene lamps were included in the top-of-the-line creations of Tiffany, Pairpoint, Handel and the foremost makers of what is known as Brilliant cut-glass. Many of the exceptional imported banquet lamps, illustrated in the section on foreign lamps, fall within that time period.

Certainly the urban wealthy would have been among the first to benefit by the introduction of electricity to their homes. There were still however, many wealthy suburban and rural residents, as well as those who had palatial winter or summer retreats, who would require expensive and opulent decor. Simultaneous production of electric, kerosene and candle lighting was carried on by many of the leading manufacturers.

The cut-glass lamps illustrated here and on p. 96 represent some of the finest examples made. Dazzling displays of cut glass from the Brilliant Period may be seen today in American museums.[1]

Banquet Lamp—All Cut Glass.
When you write, please mention "The Cosmopolitan"

Courtesy, Henry Ford Museum, The Edison Institute

Dorflinger's American Cut Glass.

A constantly increasing variety of cut glass for the table, and all ornamental purposes.

No piece genuine without our trade mark label.

C. Dorflinger & Sons,
New York.

Courtesy, The Corning Museum of Glass, Corning, New York.

a. Cut-glass lamp circa 1890-1895; probably T.G. Hawkes & Co. Corning, N.Y. Height: 35.71 inches.

Courtesy, Lightner Museum, St. Augustine, Florida

a. The five signed component parts of this cut-glass lamp identify the maker as the Libbey Glass Co. Toledo, Ohio. Approximately 39'' to the top of chimney. Circa 1900.

b. Slender composite cut-glass lamp. This lamp would have had a shade, but not necessarily a matching glass one. Height: 24'' to the top of collar.

All-Glass Lamps

c. All-glass banquet lamp.

d. to i. Cover Photograph

Relatively few all-glass banquet lamps were made. Tall composite lamps made in two or more pieces would have been easier to manufacture and ship.

The example above with opaque white blown font and base has an applied gilded ribbon encircling the base. Decorative handles also gilded are applied to the font. Both the body and shade have a polychrome painted, enamelled and gilded decoration that includes flowers, scrolls and netting.

This lamp and other similar examples in the Chrysler Museum at Norfolk, are attributed to the Mt. Washington Glass Company.

The cover photograph, lamps (d) to (i) includes both composite and all-glass lamps. The identification of these examples will serve to conclude the composite lamp section and introduce the section on all-glass lamps.

d. Painted and enamelled font with geometric design. The choice of colors, the design and the combination of font and base make this lamp an oddity (see p. 28 d).

e. Opalescent Dots and Crosses. This lamp belongs to the Mix and Match group illustrated in OL I pp. 220-224. It is combined with a Chevron stem and Round Ribbed base. (See p. 117 and p. 120.)

f. Atterbury & Co. footed hand lamp in blue and white alabaster glass. This lamp is illustrated and described in their catalogue as "No. 15 Patent Lamp, Amber Foot Lamps." This rare example is particularly valuable as an indication of the glass made by this famous lamp manufacturer during the late 1870's. Atterbury patents are described in OL I.

g. Leaf and Jewel, Opalescent Coin Dot. For related lamps, see p. 122 d and OL I pp. 276-277.

h. Allover Shells. Opalescent blue font with some shading due to the thickness of the glass. Colorless all-glass lamps were made in this pattern. They were combined with scalloped bases.

i. Heart lamp in opaque green glass. Other forms of this lamp are pictured and described on p. 103 and in OL I p. 260.

a. Shield and Star

b. Shield with Diagonal Bars

c. Prisms and Diamond Point

d. Tapered Rib

e. Fine Ribs Scalloped

f. Triple Flute and Bar

g. Swirled Segments and Vine

h. Vine and Rib

Included in this selection of flat hand lamps are several made in other forms, some of which are illustrated elsewhere in this book and in OL I.

a. Shield and Star stand lamps with this pattern are shown in the Russell and Erwin catalogue on p. 149 and in OL I p. 105.

b. Shield with Diagonal Bars is a better designed and molded version of a popular 1860's motif.[1]

c. Prisms and Diamond Point. This well-known 1860's lamp pattern was made for composite lamps with fair-to-poor quality mold-blown fonts (OL I p. 164 f); and in excellent quality pressed fonts. (p. 78 f).

d. Tapered Rib. See p. 71 h and the Russell and Erwin catalogue example on p. 149 for composite lamps with inverted fonts.

e. Fine Ribs Scalloped. Like (d) this pattern could easily be inverted and used for a stand lamp. Two of these lamps have had original use in Ontario.

f. Triple Flute and Bar. Rare flat hand form of the well-known 1860's pattern. Several examples of stand lamps are illustrated in this book, OL I and the Dietz catalogue.

g. Swirled Segments and Vine. My records include a photograph of a blue lamp with an Oakleaf Bubble base (OL I p. 292 d) and a font essentially the same as this. The main difference is that while the segments swirl in the same direction, the vine is reversed.

h. Vine and Rib. The early collar and general appearance of this lamp suggest manufacture in the early 1870's.

i. Diagonal Rib and Pod. Other forms of this lamp of the early 1870's are shown in OL I.

j. Diagonal Rib and Pod. The post-1876 collar and awkward molded handle suggest a later modification of the example (i).

k. Prisms with Plain Band. This relatively common lamp, probably of the 1880's and 90's, was also made in opaque white and possibly in colors.

l. Diamond and Scroll. See p. 82 c.

i. Diagonal Rib and Pod

j. Diagonal Rib and Pod

k. Prisms with Plain Band

l. Diamond and Scroll

m. Banded Prism.

n. Zipper and Rib

o. Brick Band

p. Fringed Curtain

q. Single Dotted Band

r. Double Dotted Band

s. Double Bullseye Band

t. Morocco

u. Triple Band and Fan

v. Daisy[ON.]

w. Concord Grape

x. Plume

m. Banded Prism. Goblet and tableware patterns of the 1880's closely resemble this lamp pattern. It was also made in a good medium blue and possibly other colors.

n. Zipper and Rib. Typical 1880's pattern, possibly made in tableware.

o. Brick Band. The Henry & Nathan Russell 1884 catalogue supplement shown in OL I pp. 214-215 offered this lamp for $1.80 per dozen. Some tableware patterns of this period include a brick or tile wall.

p. Fringed Curtain. Advertised by French, Potter & Wilson, wholesalers in 1880[1] and described as "a good hand lamp to retail for 25 cents." In assorted colors of crystal, amber and blue, it sold for $1.12 per dozen with No. 1 burners included.

q. Single Dotted Band. Simple pattern probably of the 1880's.

r. Double Dotted Band. Similar to *(q)*.

s. Double Bullseye Band. Interesting pattern circa 1890. The handle is pressed.

t. Morocco. Lamp with large looping applied handle, probably 1880's.

u. Triple Band and Fan. Goblets were made in this 1880's pattern.[2]

v. Daisy.[ON] Three stand lamps and this flat hand lamp were illustrated in an undated Westmoreland Specialty Company advertisement.[3] The squat version illustrated on p. 119 i is not shown. Known to have been made in opaque white and blue and possibly other colors, it is a favorite of Midwest collectors today.

w. Concord Grape. This pattern was made with and without a roughed surface on the raised grapes and leaves. The matching stand lamp has a plain stem and round base.

x. Plume. Manufacture of the Plume tableware pattern in the 1870's and 1880's is attributed to Adams & Company, Pittsburgh, PA.[4] This lamp appears to be a product of the 1880's.

a.

b.

c.

e.

f.

g.

h.

i.

j.

k.

l.

m.

a. The blown bracket or hanging lamp font in blue has had a free-formed stem and base added to make a stand lamp.

b. Grant^ON also in dark blue has a base that relates to lamps illustrated in OL I p. 117.

c. Flute and Block is related to lamps in OL I p. 263.

d. Today this Lion lamp is considered very rare by collectors and yet they were undoubtedly produced in large quantities. The catalogue information supplied is very interesting; particularly the price.

e. An article by Ann Gilbert McDonald[1] featuring lamps made by Dithridge & Co. Pittsburgh, PA illustrates three lamps advertised in 1900. Included were two vase lamps with variations of the design on this lamp and on one shown in OL I p. 257. Other examples of (e) have been seen with various accent colors on the frills. A crudely finished variation in colorless glass, was completely frosted, except for the areas around the flowers. Other pieces, advertised in the April 5, 1900 issue of China, Glass and Lamps, were named Versailles.[2]

f. A rather commonplace lamp, circa 1900, becomes extraordinary when made with opalescent glass.

g. This patterned and painted lamp was also made by Dithridge & Co. Other examples have been seen with pink as the base color.

h. Queen Heart. An opaque white squat version of these popular lamps illustrated in OL I.

i. & j. Swirl and Depressed Daisy bases. The rose font (i) has a drip-catcher and the font (j) is plain with ribbing at the base.

k. Bullseye lamps with opaque white or blue glass bases are keenly sought after by collectors. Several forms are illustrated in OL I p. 270.

l. Sultan^ON in Chocolate Glass. See p. 103 for other names and information.

m. Four Seasons. Four females and four seasons are depicted on the panels of this font. Plain colored stand and footed hand lamps were also made. The base is similar to Margo illustrated in OL I p. 290 e.

a.

b.

c.

d.

e.

f.

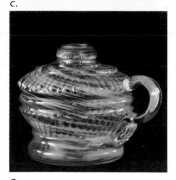
g.

h.

i.

j.

k.

l.

m.

n.

o.

p.

Sixteen different flat and footed hand lamps are pictured here. They are typical of the colored varieties made between 1860 and 1900.

a. Masonic. This deep amethyst blown font, with large looped applied handle, has a pattern around the base that includes Masonic Lodge symbols. Circa 1860.

b. Pyramid and Palm. Blown font with applied handle. This pattern has also been seen on bracket and hanging lamp fonts. 1860's.

c. Polka Dot. This opalescent optic molded design in clear, blue or cranberry is also found on footed hand and stand lamps. See OL I pp. 236-237 No. 6 and also (j) below.

d. Hobbs Dots. An optic molded version of the well-known opalescent Hobbs Coin Dot Lamps.

e. Diamond Band and Shield. Also made in blue and colorless, (see OL I p. 102 b).

f. Seaweed. See p. 104 for other examples and description.

g. Bloxam flat hand lamp form of stand lamp p. 104 g.

h. Emma. Optic molded lamp of the 1880's with applied handle.

i. Network. Unusual patterned colorless mold-blown font with pressed blue base and handle. Probably 1880's.

j. Angela. This lamp was made in different color combinations. Lamps in OL I p. 236 No. 6 and p. 273 h suggest the possibility that this lamp is related to (c) above.

k. Opalescent Coin Dot lamp with unusual pressed handle.

l. Markham Swirl Band with Opalescent Cobweb. Markham Swirl lamps were made in different forms with various opalescent designs, in white, blue, cranberry and possibly yellow. See OL I p. 280 and pp. 234-235 for named and unnamed examples.

m. Venetian[ON] (see p. 123 j.). $2.25 per doz. in 1881.[1]

n. Eason. Footed hand lamp form of the lamp shown in OL I pp. 236-237 No. 4, bottom row.

o. Diamond and Fan. This pattern was also made in a stand lamp form. It was also made in amber, and possibly other colors.

p. Cup and Saucer. The most common of all saucer-base lamps; usually found in colorless glass, (see OL I p. 196 c).[2]

a.

b.

c. Detail, handle of lamp (b)

d.

e.

f.

g.

h.

i.

a. Butterfly and Anchor. The footed hand-lamp form of a popular lamp pattern, that is found with or without a frosted finish on the font. In addition to butterflies and anchors, there are bells and horseshoes. Certainly a mixed bag! See also p. 122 h and OL I p. 271 l.

b. Allover Stars. Made in 1880's by the Central Glass Company, Wheeling, WV and later by the United States Glass Company. It was available in clear, blue and amber (shown).

The gaffer who finished this lamp left an unusual mark. A tool with a chevron design was frequently used to press the end of an applied handle against the body of the piece. Each design varied to some degree and became the maker's individual mark. The owl (c) is a rare mark to watch for.

d. Melon with Fine Rib. Hand lamps of this type without a separate glass foot, could be referred to as semi-footed. See also p. 75 j and p. 110 d. Height: 4-1/4''.

e. One-piece Loop. Although similar to the one-piece lamps of the 1890's, this lamp is most commonly found with a pre-1876 type of collar. Some of these lamps may date from the late 1870's. Height: 5-3/4''.

f. Dart. Pressed footed hand-lamp form of the stand lamp illustrated in OL I p. 298 c. Tableware pieces were made in this pattern. Height: 4-1/4''.

g. Duncan Ribbed Band. A one-piece, two-handled footed hand-lamp form of the stand lamp shown in OL I p. 316 a. It was illustrated in two sizes (4-3/4'' and 5-1/4'') in the United States Glass Company catalogue. Tableware pieces are attributed to George Duncan & Sons, Pittsburgh, PA. Height: 4-3/4''.

h. Riverside Rib and Plain Band. See OL I p. 243 e for the stand-lamp form. Advertised as one of a new line in 1889, it was described as "something handsome".

i. Riverside Rondo. This is the footed hand-lamp form of the lamps shown in OL I, p. 247 d. Height: 4-5/8''.

j. Hero.[ON] The name Pillow Encircled has been used to describe two similar patterns advertised in the Montgomery Ward & Co. 1894 catalogue.[1] The pattern on lamp *(j)* was called Hero; and the other called Midway was almost identical except for a straight groove across the top of the patterned band.

An article by William Heacock[2] includes an advertisement by the West Virginia Glass Mfg. Co. showing a different footed hand lamp with the Hero pattern on the font and base, and with a different handle. Heacock notes that he has seen it in a shade of cobalt blue that matches the color of West Virginia's Optic pattern. The Hero stand lamp has been seen in green, blue and clear with an optic-molded, ribbed font. Height: 5''.

This footed hand lamp with its dramatic double loop handle may be another variation made by the West Virginia Glass Mfg. Co. Martins Ferry, OH.

k. Sultan.[ON] I called this lamp Wild Rose and Bowknot in OL I; the name commonly used. Tableware and other glass patterns were occasionally modified when adapted for oil lamps, but nevertheless retained the name of the related pieces for identification. James Measell calls this lamp pattern Wild Rose and Festoon, although he states the original name given to it by McKee was Sultan.[3] By any other name the lamp would be highly collectable!

l. Dominion Panel. This lamp is an interesting addition to the Mix and Match related lamps illustrated in OL I pp. 220-224. The applied handle is an unusual variation.

m. King Melon Optic. This pattern with opalescent spots is called Dot Opalescent[ON] in the King Glass Co. Pittsburgh, catalogue 1885-1891.[4] This colorless example has a rather strange but interesting appearance. See p. 116 b for the colored Dot Opalescent stand-lamp form.

n. Daisy and Bowknot. The 1903 Cambridge Glass, Co. Cambridge, Ohio, catalogue illustrates this lamp, along with a flat hand lamp and five different sizes of stand lamps. Height: 5''.

o. Ellipse with Thumbprint. This lamp is related to the Heart Lamp on the cover and p. 97, as well as lamps in OL I p. 260. *Tarentum Pattern Glass* by Robert Irwin Lucas has illustrations and information that relate to these lamps.[5]

Two patterns, Heart and Thumbprint and Princeton, made by the Tarentum Glass Co. bear some resemblance to these related lamps. This company also made opaque custard and green glass. Also in Lucas' book is a Richards & Hartley Glass Co. advertisement, showing two footed hand lamps with handles and fonts like those in this related group. Height: 4-5/8''.

p. Prince Edward. The footed hand-lamp form of the popular 1890's pattern. See page 125 g. Height: 5-3/8''.

q. Princess Feather. The handle of this footed hand lamp is an uncommon variation of the one pictured in OL I p. 279. Height: 5-1/2''.

j.

k.

l.

m.

n.

o.

p.

q.

a. & b.

d.

e.

f.

g.

h.

i.

c.

a. & b. Optic Opalescent Seaweed. Bowls, bitters and barber bottles, as well as other glassware in this pattern, were advertised by the Beaumont Glass Co., Martins Ferry, OH, between 1895 and 1905.[1] Clear glass lamps in this design however, were advertised in the United States Glass Company catalogue, circa 1893 and in a miniature form in their 1909 catalogue. The molds for these lamps may have been readily available to any company.

c. Hobbs Snowflake.[2] Flat hand lamp form.

d. Ringed Base with opalescent striped font.

e. Jensen with opalescent striped font. See p. 109 for other examples.

f. Plain round base with opalescent stripe.

g. Bloxam with opalescent striped font. This lamp was made with spatter fonts in pink and white and in blue and white. Another example has been seen with both base and font in an unusual deep teal blue.

h. Alva. Many variations of this lamp were made. A colorless-glass ribbed version is illustrated in OL I p. 271. Another colorless example, without ribbing, was made with a frosted band and base. Two other variations are illustrated on p. 117.

i. Banbury. In 1888 a colorless glass lamp with this base and a slightly different font, was advertised by the "NICKEL-PLATE GLASS CO., FOSTORIO, OHIA [sic]". This Fostoria company also advertised opalescent glassware.[3]

Opposite ▷

Opalescent blue variations of lamps illustrated elsewhere in this book and in OL I. They are, left to right, Sheldon Swirl, Hobbs Coin Dot, Venice[ON], and Mix and Match with Chevron stem and Round Ribbed Base. Note the different detail below the font on the Hobbs Coin Dot lamp. All of the lamps on these two pages were made between 1885 and 1905

a. Ring and Rib

b. Checkered Star Band

c. Hamilton with Leaf

d. York

e. Allover Bullseye

f. Panelled Bullseye

g. Triple Flute and Bar

h. Ring Punty

i. Honeycomb

a. Ring and Rib. This lamp was displayed at the Great North American Kerosene Lamp Exhibit at the Huntington Galleries in Huntington WV in 1983. It was placed beside an Argus and a Bohemian celery holder, with an open Bakewell, Pears Co. catalogue circa 1875, illustrating the celery holders. All bases appeared to be the same and although comparison for identical mold characteristics had not been made, it seems probable that the three pieces were made by this Pittsburgh company.

b. Checkered Star Band. Small stand lamp circa 1870. Height: 6-1/2''.

c. Hamilton with Leaf. This tableware pattern is described by Kamm as a lighter and later version of the Hamilton pattern.[1] The only other example of this 1870's lamp that I have seen had a base with fifteen scallops. 7'' high.

d. York. Small stand lamp circa 1870.

e. Allover Bullseye. Other examples I have seen of this pattern have had the same problem. The pattern almost disappears in certain areas of the font.

Lamps (f), (g), (h) & (i) have well-known pressed fonts, combined with pressed bases that have not been illustrated before in these combinations.

f. Panelled Bullseye. Pressed base with eight large scallops.

g. Triple Flute and Bar and h. Ring Punty are combined with fluted and scalloped bases that could be the same. They were photographed at two different locations and were not available for comparison. Height: (h) 7-1/8''.

i. Honeycomb. This base appears to be an early form of the Oval Band base patented in 1871 by John Oesterling (see OL I pp. 204-206).

j. M'Kee Tulip is the lamp that was illustrated in their 1864 and 1868 catalogues (see p. 31). This font combined with an opaque white base is called Ribbed Tulip in OL I. The glass quality is very good and the lamp is considerably more attractive than the catalogue illustration indicates. On plate No. 8 of the Dietz catalogue, No. 895 appears to have this Tulip font.

Courtesy, Huntington Galleries, Huntington, WV

k. Columbia. This base probably represents Columbia, although not too favorably. The font pattern appears to conform to the David Barker 1877 design patent, assigned to the Crystal Glass Company of Pittsburgh.[1] This is good but not infallible evidence for attribution.

A compote with this base was also made in opaque white and in purple Marble glass; probably by Challinor Taylor & Co., Tarentum, PA., circa 1900.[2]

a. & b. Picket stand and miniature lamps with a complex geometric pattern. Examples of these lamps, circa 1890, are usually found in good quality colorless or amber glass. The handle of this miniature and the footed hand lamp (c) appear to have the same design.

c. Match Holder Rib Font. See p. 117 for fonts of this same design combined with match holder bases. An irregularity that occurred during the pressing probably caused the flaw in the handle. Circa 1890.

d. Picket. Amber stain and engraving accent the plain panels of this lamp. Also made with amber stain on other parts of the lamp.

e. Hobbs Frances Ware. The combination of amber stain and frosted glass was used on many articles of glassware made by the Hobbs, Brockunier & Company. It was named after the wife of President Cleveland.

f. Hobbs Ringed Hobnail, also made by Hobbs, Brockunier & Company. The rings surrounding the hobs create an optical effect that is very different from other hobnail lamps. Circa 1890.

g. & h. Basketweave with Medallions. Footed hand and stand lamp with one of the most complex patterns found on a lamp.

i. Sheldon Swirl. The bright gold effect on this font was created by silvering the inside of a transparent amber font. Little remains of the silver in most examples of these lamps. A silver coating was also applied to colorless lamps giving them a bright silver appearance.

j. & k. Jensen beaded base with opalescent striped font. Footed hand lamp and stand lamp examples in amber. See p. 104 e for an example with a blue base.

l. Central Hobnail. This lamp was made by the Central Glass Company in Wheeling, WV in the 1880's. They used this base in combination with other fonts.

m. Dogtooth and Panel. Many examples of this footed hand lamp have been seen in amber and colorless glass. Circa 1890.

n. Raymond Swirl. The illustration of this lamp in the United States Glass Company catalogue circa 1893, shows the pattern swirling in the opposite direction. It may have been made earlier by the Central Glass Company, Wheeling, WV or the Bellaire Goblet Co. at Findlay, OH.

o. Most of the one-piece pressed glass lamps of the 1890's were made in colorless glass, but a few were made in blue and amber. The drip-catcher on this lamp is similar to those on the Lomax lamps.

p. Courter. This patterned font has been seen on a stand lamp with a base that relates to the Columbian Coin lamps.

q. Depressed Oval Bands. A very different example of this lamp was made with a colorless base and a cranberry opalescent lattice-design font.

r. Optic Band. The footed hand lamp form of this lamp is very unusual. The font is the same but the base is a ribbed conical form.

g.

h.

i.

j.

k.

l.

m.

n.

o.

p.

q.

r.

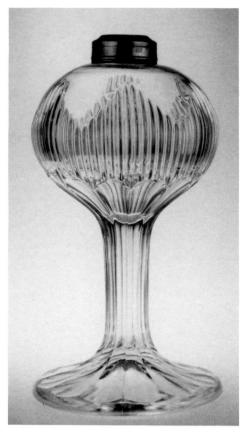

a. Icicle & Panel

b. One-piece Thumbprint

c. Late Thumbprint

d. Melon and Fine Rib

e. Woodvine

f. Double Diamond Cluster

g. Rochelle[ON]

h. Feathered Bullseye and
Fleur-de-lis.

i. Periwinkle

a. Icicle & Panel. A one-piece lamp with lead content. The design is clean. An icicle pattern springs from panels that continue down the stem and radiate outwards to the edge of the foot.

b. One-piece Thumbprint. The font, fire polished as it was drawn in to form a neck, could easily be mistaken for lead glass, however, sound and sight tell us the base of this one-piece lamp is unleaded.

c. Late Thumbprint. A clumsy lamp circa 1900 or later, that appears to be an attempt to imitate the characteristics of lamps (a) and (b). Like so many imitations, it was a failure.

d. Melon and Fine Rib. Examination of similar all-glass lamps with opaque white fonts and blue bases, has revealed definite differences. See also pp. 75 j, 102 d and OL I p. 203 f.

e. Woodvine. This simple pattern was probably made during the early 1870's.

f. Double Diamond Cluster and Loop. A mold-blown example in a typical pressed design.

g. Rochelle.[ON] This pattern is also called Princess Feather, however, use of the original name will avoid confusion with the popular Princess Feather lamps made at a later date. Goblets, compotes and other tableware pieces in this pattern were illustrated in the Bakewell, Pears & Co. Pittsburgh catalogue circa 1875. Neither the base of this lamp, nor the scroll above the pattern, appears on any of the catalogue pieces. This evidence indicates the possibility that another company made Rochelle lamps.

h. Feathered Bullseye and Fleur-de-lis. A mold-blown example of the well-known pressed pattern. This one is illustrated in Russell and Erwin (see p. 149), and in the Dietz catalogue.

i. Periwinkle. A conventional form of the pattern shown also on p. 67 f. A Ring Punty font is shown with this base in OL I p. 84 b.

Sizes are: (a) 7-5/8'', (b) 8'', (c) 8-1/8'', (d) 7-1/2'', (e) 7-7/8'', (f) 7-1/8'', (g) 10-1/2'', (h) 8-1/8'' (i) 7-7/8''.

j. Riverside Ring and Rib

k. Cable and Oval

l. Greensburg 200

j. Riverside Ring and Rib. The Riverside Glass Company added variety to their line by interchanging fonts and bases. New combinations continue to come to light. This lamp of the 1880's has the good proportions and quality of most Riverside lamps. 8-1/4" high.

k. Cable and Oval. Mold-blown font with cable design repeated on the pressed base. Probably 1880's. Height: 9-1/2".

l. Greensburg 200. The Greensburg Glass Co., Greensburg, PA advertised this lamp with a different stem and its matching footed hand lamp numbered 200 in 1890.[1] Their counterparts with plain fonts were numbered 201. Ribbing is repeated from the deep drip-depression through the font stem and on the base. Height: 8-1/8".

m. Sheffield Swirl. Swirled design typical of the 1880's. Height: 8-3/4".

n. Daisy and Scroll. This is another design that was probably made in the 1880's. 8-7/8" high.

o. Ball Base Swirl. Some tableware pieces were made with bases similar to this. See also Findlay Ball Base lamp OL I p. 254. 7-7/8" high.

p. Bevelled Blocks. Well-defined mold-blown font with pattern repeated on the base. Probably 1880's.

q. Riverside Arms. The patterned arm-like handles are more decorative and interesting than useful on this lamp with a Riverside collar.

r. Jewel Clusters. Mold-blown font with a strange type of greyish spatter on the base.

m. Sheffield Swirl

n. Daisy and Scroll

o. Ball Base Swirl

p. Bevelled Blocks

q. Riverside Arms

r. Jewel Clusters

a. & b. In OL I p. 263, I called two lamp designs Carlisle and numbered them 1 and 4. Sequential attribution links them to the two lamps, Carlisle 2 and 3, shown here.

An article by Ann Gilbert McDonald[1] illustrated another related miniature lamp, the McKee No. 122. I will refer to it as Carlisle 5. It has the font of Carlisle 3 and 4, combined with the base of Carlisle 1. At the same time that I named the two lamps in OL I Carlisle, Bill Heacock gave the name Reflecting Fans to a cruet with a pattern similar to that on the base of the lamps pictured here.[2]

Because these lamps are sequentially related, and since there is no design feature common to all, I prefer to continue to use the family name Carlisle as a unifying factor to easily identify and relate this group.

From information in Kamm V, McDonald concludes that the Reflecting Fans lamp (Smith 480) was made by both the Belmont Glass Works in Bellaire, OH, and by McKee and Brothers in Pittsburgh, PA. See also p. 154.

a. Carlisle 2

b. Carlisle 3

c. A Consolidated Lamp and Glass Co. advertisement in 1894, illustrated the tall lamp (c), named Princess, with a fancy shade "trimmed with silk."

Florette, the collector's name for this lamp, is the name I used in OL I.

d. & e. Quilt[ON] was the name given to this pattern by the maker, Consolidated Lamp and Glass Co. Pittsburgh, PA.[1] These lamps were also illustrated in the same catalogue as the lamps shown on p. 92. The pattern was described as "Quilt, yellow, cased colors." The other colors would have been rose and blue. The Montgomery Ward & Co. 1895 catalogue No. 57 advertised the Quilt caster set in rose and turquoise blue for 75¢.

c. Princess   d. Quilt[ON]

e. Quilt[ON]

a. Roulette

b. Thompson No. 77

c. Skedden

d. Elite[ON]

e. Oklahoma[ON]

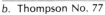

f. Thumbprint Hex Block

g. Artichoke

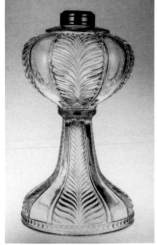

h. Feathered Panel

i. Co-op No. 323

a. Roulette. The font, stem and base of this lamp are covered with a busy design that has borrowed many characteristics from earlier days. Height: 8-1/2''.

b. Thompson No. 77. Tableware pieces in this pattern were advertised in the Pottery and Glassware Reporter in 1891.[1] Height: 8-1/4''.

Two lamps made by the Thompson Glass Co. Uniontown, PA are illustrated in the 1903 Cambridge Glass Co. catalogue, with patterned bases and plain fonts (see p. 122).

c. Skedden. The font and base patterns of this lamp are completely unrelated. This suggests these parts may appear in other combinations. Probably 1880's. Height: 8-5/8''.

d. Elite.[ON] See (e) below. Height: 9-1/4''.

e. Oklahoma.[ON] The Elite lamp (d) and the font of Oklahoma combined with another base, are illustrated in an 1890 advertisement of the Dalzell, Gilmore & Leighton Co. Findlay, OH.[2] Height: 9''.

Two other lamps are illustrated and they clearly show a sequential relationship between lamps (d) and (e). Cross Lens, the name I used in OL I, is the name given to the Oklahoma pattern by author Don Smith.

f. Thumbprint Hex Block. Shards of a footed hand lamp with this font pattern, were found at Findlay, OH. It has been attributed to the Findlay Flint Glass Company by Don E. Smith.[3] Height: 9-1/4''.

g. Artichoke. The Fostoria Glass Co. Fostoria, OH advertised eight of these lamps in 1891, all numbered 205 and described as ''our latest pattern''.[4] Height: 9''.

h. Feathered Panel. This lamp, made also in a squat form, was produced in opaque white and colored glass. Height: 10-1/2''.

i. Co-op No. 323. Tableware pieces of this pattern were advertised in 1905. Approx. 9-1/2''.

j.

k.

l.

j. Cooper. This lamp was advertised in 1888 by French, Potter & Wilson, a wholesale company in Chicago.[1] It was listed in clear glass in four sizes 8'', 9'', 9-1/2'' and 10-1/2''.

k. Fishscale and Panelled Band. This is possibly the most realistic of the many fishscale patterns.

l. Diamonds Reversed. The diamonds on the font of this lamp are slightly raised and those on the stem are concave.

Lamps (j), (k) and (l) have mold-blown fonts and pressed bases. Lamps (m) to (r) have been pressed in one piece. Lamps of this type, popular in the 1890's are heavy and generally of very good quality.

m. Riven Ribs. Both quality and design of this lamp are well above average.

n. Bevelled Panels. Heavy squat form with drip-catcher flange. Brilliant fire-polished glass.

o. Fingerprints. Excellent quality lamp that was also made in the footed hand-lamp form.

p. Carlaw. A plain lamp with scalloped flange.

q. One-piece Colonial. Another squat heavy lamp similar to (n).

r. Burne. This pattern is similar to many goblet and tableware patterns of the 1880's and 90's.

m.

n.

o.

p.

q.

r.

a.

b.

c.

d.

e.

f.

g.

h.

i.

j.

k.

l.

Many of the lamps illustrated here are colored examples or variations of ones illustrated elsewhere in this book or in OL I.

a. Princess Feather. This version with an orange font is one of the most sought-after of the very popular Princess Feather lamps. The pattern was originally made by the Consolidated Lamp Co., and later by other glass companies.

b. King Melon with Opalescent Spots. This lamp was advertised by King Glass Co. Pittsburgh, PA, in 1890 and by the United States Glass Company in their catalogue circa 1893. Other forms of this lamp are illustrated in OL I and in this book on p. 103.

c. Fraser. A plain lamp, probably made in the twentieth century.

d. Princess Feather. Opaque turquoise in the tall stand-lamp form. Most of the opaque-glass Princess Feather lamps were made in the squat form.

e. Prince Edward. Stand lamp with cased yellow font and clear base.

f. Prince Edward. Squat form of the Prince Edward lamp in blue opaque glass.

g. Rosa. A twentieth-century lamp made in a semi-automatic machine.

h. Shane. The difference in thickness between the mold-blown font and pressed base, makes the two parts appear to be a different color. Circa 1890.

i. Diamond Quilt. This lamp has a diamond pattern optic-molded font with a drip depression. Circa 1890.

j. X and O. This lamp is related to one illustrated in the United States Glass Company catalogue circa 1893; and to two in OL I p. 314.

k. Colin. Plain opaque white lamp, probably made during the 1890's.

l. Bassett. Transparent blue glass plain utilitarian lamp; probably of the 1890's.

m. & n.

o. & p.

m. & n. Match Holder Base lamps. Two lamps advertised by French, Potter & Wilson[1] are the same as those illustrated above and the one in OL I p. 283 i. The latter has a painted leaf design on a plain font. These interesting lamps have a match striker as well as a place to hold the matches. On two of the vertical sides of each base there is a series of fine corrugations that serve as the strikers. One would have to be very dextrous to use it without scorching the table.

o. & p. Alva. Two examples of a lamp that was made with many variations and in different colors. See also p. 104 h.

q. r. s. & t. Mix and Match. This large group of related lamps is illustrated in OL I. Some were advertised in the United States Glass Company catalogue circa 1893. King Glass Co. of Pittsburgh, who made King Melon colored lamps with opalescent dots, also made Mix and Match lamps with Chevron stems, Round Ribbed Bases and Feather Duster fonts. It is probable that they also made these lamps.

The opalescent areas on *(q)* almost obscure the pale yellow color of the lamp. It is unusual for the opalescence to extend down into the stem of the lamp. *(r),* also shown on the cover, is included here for comparison. Because of the method of manufacture, there is a great deal of variation in the appearance of the spots and in the opacity of the area surrounding them. This is evident in the examples illustrated here.

Lamp *(s)* in amber, is deeper and more reddish than the example *(t)*.

q.

r.

s.

t.

a. Buffalo. Four well-detailed buffalo heads are the focal point of this colorless lamp. It was also made in amber and has been reported with other animal heads.

b. Hyla with Star. This frosted font includes a Star of David and stylized flowers in the corners. Flat Oval Window, OL I p. 280 i, is the plain flat hand-lamp form.

c. Riverside 300. Riverside Glassworks, Wellsburg, WV advertised this lamp in 1888. The solid stem with bevelled blocks, was used on tableware pieces made by Riverside.

d. Hanging Baskets. This well-detailed font has a band of medallions with hanging baskets filled with flowers. Probably 1880's.

e. Fantasia. Japanese and Egyptian designs, especially popular in the 1880's and 1890's, are featured on the font and foot of this lamp.

f. Hobnail-Double Eye. This very rare form of two-piece glass vase lamp is almost identical to a pitcher attributed to the Columbia Glass Company, Findlay, OH.[1]

g. Fostoria Icicle. This lamp and one with a plain font, was advertised in 1889 by the Fostoria Glass Co.[1] They were numbered D. 153 and D. 154 respectively. Superior detail and glass quality.

h. Wheel and Comma. The Aetna Glass and Mfg. Co. Bellaire, OH advertised this pattern in 1881-3.[2] This superior quality lamp, with its absurd handles, may have been made at a later date.

i. Daisy.ON Manufactured by the Westmoreland Specialty Co. in the 1890's, in colorless, opaque white and colored glass. See p. 99 v for the flat hand lamp and additional information.

j. Lion and Baboon. An amusing lamp in a known tableware pattern.[3] Similar to Princess Feather of the 1890's but could have been made much later. Lions are on the font and baboons on the foot.

a. Aquarius lamps

b. Mix and Match lamps

c. Sheldon Swirl lamps

Colorless-glass examples of the lamps on these two pages are described and illustrated in OL I. The range of color and types of glass, give the collector an idea of what was available at the time these lamps were made, and what might be available today.

a. Aquarius lamps. This pattern was advertised in the 1880's and 90's. The group shown here includes two shades of blue, amber, vaseline or yellow, an unusual shade of brown, and turquoise. Together they make an interesting group. Note the lamp on the far left has a round base. These are much less common than the scalloped-base lamps.

b. Mix and Match lamps. A selection of striped and dotted lamps.

c. Sheldon Swirl lamps. Examples of striped and spattered glass in this popular pattern.

Opposite ▷
Carnival glass lamps. This iridescent glass was produced primarily in the early twentieth century by Midwest glass companies. It was so named because of its popularity as a "give-away" at Carnivals; but not today!

d. Zipper Loop. A resist was used on the clear parts to achieve selective areas of gold.

e. Marigold Zipper Loop. This vibrant color was the most popular one used on lamps.

f. Squat Zipper Loop. The technique used to make carnival glass produced not only iridescence but many shades as well.

g. Wild Rose. See OL I p. 246 for an earlier colorless example.

d. Zipper Loop

e. Marigold Zipper Loop

f. Squat Zipper Loop

g. Wild Rose

a.

b.

c.

d.

e.

f.

g.

h.

i.

All of the lamps on this page are related to lamps illustrated in OL I.

a. Squirrel with Cuffed Hand and Torch base. Squirrel (OL I p. 271 h), is combined here with a variation of the Hand and Torch base illustrated in OL I p. 278. Height: 9-1/8''.

b. Scrolled Acanthus with Francis Base. See OL I p. 296 for an example with a different font. These lamps made by The Fostoria Glass Co. have bases that closely resemble Fostoria's Priscilla pattern. Fostoria, nearing its 100th anniversary was one of the largest manufacturers of kerosene lamps, particularly vase lamps. Height: 9-1/8''.

c. Stippled Daisy and Leaf Band with Scallops and Fan. This variation of the lamp in OL I p. 201 j, has a pattern below the band, as well as a different base. The base of the lamp in OL I also appears on another lamp with a matching font pattern. Identification of one part will give us the attribution for three lamps. Height: 9''.

d. Double Leaf and Jewel. This is a pleasing variation of the blue opalescent cover lamp (see p. 97), and of the lamp Leaf and Jewel in OL I, pp. 276-277. Height: 9-5/8''.

e. Belmont with Daisy and Button. This lamp has the Daisy and Button pattern shown on the matching tableware pieces (see OL I p. 288). Height: 7-1/8''.

f. Delaware.[ON] See OL I pp. 248-249 for related lamps made by Dalzell, Gilmore and Leighton in Findlay, OH. Height: 8''.[1]

g. Torpedo. This lamp is illustrated in the 1903 Cambridge Glass Company catalogue. The Torpedo lamp with matching font in OL I pp. 290-291, was probably made by the Thompson Glass Co. Limited, Uniontown, PA who advertised this tableware pattern in 1899.[2] Height: 10-1/4''.

h. Butterfly and Anchor Base. This lamp has also been seen with a frosted base and stem. See p. 102 a and OL I p. 271 l for lamps with the patterned font. Height: 10-3/8''.

i. Carlton Medallion. See OL I p. 296 a for an example with matching font. Height: 9-3/4''.

j. Venice.[ON] French, Potter and Wilson described this "beautiful new style of glass lamps" in 1888.[1] Their advertisement included a footed hand lamp they called Venetian[ON] (see p. 101 m) and a hand-painted variation called Grecian[ON] *(figs. 1 & 2).* They also offered a "Venetian Assortment" that included each model, complete with burners and chimneys.

The Venice stand lamps were sold with clear or blue opalescent striped fonts and frosted bases (see p. 105). The sizes and wholesale prices were:

No. 1, 8" with No. 1 burner ... $4.00 per doz.
No. 2, 9" with No. 1 burner ... $5.00 per doz.
No. 3, 10" with No. 2 burner ... $6.50 per doz.

The Grecian hand-painted style was listed at $5.00, $6.50 and $8.50 for the respective sizes. These prices included burners and fancy chimneys!

In OL I p 268 the yellow or vaseline example called Gay Opalescent was either made later, or sold through a different outlet.

The footed Venetian hand lamp is very similar to the Eason hand lamp p. 101 n. The most obvious differences are the font shoulders, the handles and the frosted base of the Venetian.

k. Dunkirk Six Panel. About two decades after the Venice lamp was introduced, many styles of inexpensive "Sewing" lamps appeared with large matching chimneys or chimney-shades as they were also called. They were made until at least the late 1920's. This one was offered in an undated catalogue of the Indiana Glass Company, Dunkirk, IN.[2] Height to top of chimney 18".

l. Pineapple and Fan or Shepherd's Plaid. Both names are used by writers and collectors. The pattern was made by the Model Flint Glass Company in Albany, Indiana sometime between 1893 and 1901 or 1902; and later by the Indiana Glass Company in Dunkirk.[3]

This lamp could have been a product of either factory, or both. Height to the top of the shade 16-1/2".

fig. 1 Venice[ON]   *fig. 2* Grecian[ON]

Table lamps with chimneys to match. "Our cut does not do the goods justice." — from the American Potter & Illuminator February, 1888.
Private Collection.

fig. 3 Mission[ON]   *fig. 4* Bellevue[ON]

Lamps illustrated in the No. 13 undated, Pittsburgh Lamp, Brass and Glass Company, Pittsburgh, PA catalogue.[4]

Courtesy, Antique & Colonial Lighting. Clarence, New York.

a. This lamp was illustrated in an Indiana Glass Company catalogue dating from 1907 through the 1930's.[1] It was described as "No. 10 F. Massive Sewing Lamp. Available with No. 2 Riverside Special Clinch Collar or Common Clinch Collar."

b. Princess Feather in this style was also advertised in the same catalogue. It was also in a Sears, Roebuck catalogue between 1905 and 1910, as well as in their 1927 catalogue, where it was decorated as above with gilded base and ruby-colored flowers.

c. With the exception of the iron base, this lamp is similar to (a) and (b). It would probably have sold around 1910 for about $1.50 instead of 67¢ for the undecorated lamp (b).

d. Inverted Thumbprint and Fan Base, dramatically illustrates the difference between lamps with matching chimneys, circa 1890, and others shown here (see OL I p. 290 d).

e. The collar on this lamp inside the glass neck of the font, is an indication that it was made in the second decade of this century or later.

f. This type of garish painted decoration, predominantly gold with bright colors, was used on many twentieth-century lamps. It is referred to as Goofus Glass.

g. Opaque green Prince Edward lamp with matching shade. I have not seen the Prince Edward lamp advertised by a manufacturer, however I have seen this shade advertised.

I am sure it will come as a surprise to lamp collectors to hear that in a 1902 Consolidated Lamp catalogue a Princess Feather lamp, in the squat form, is illustrated with this shade.[1] Consolidated very likely sold shades separately and they were probably bought and sold with an eye to matching color rather than matching design. On p. 92 there are two Consolidated Lamp Co. banquet lamps with shades that do not repeat the pattern of the base.

h. Bellevue.[ON] This lamp was named in the catalogue of the Pittsburgh Lamp, Brass and Glass company, Pittsburgh, PA. It is shown with a matching shade as well as in five sizes of stand lamps, a footed hand lamp and a flat hand lamp. These are all illustrated in OL I pp. 280-281. Coolidge Drape is the name commonly given to this lamp because of its presence in the room when President Coolidge took the oath of office. See also p. 123.

g. Prince Edward

h. Bellevue[ON]

Foreign Lamps

Despite distances and difficulties, imports and exports of china, glass and lamps were a viable part of the nineteenth century marketplace. England and continental Europe as well as the United States supplied most of the world with kerosene lamps. They also supplied each other with the most ordinary and the most elegant examples. Many of those that were shipped to other parts of the world are described and illustrated in *Oil & Kerosene Lamps in Australia* by Peter Cuffley.

This book includes hundreds of catalogue illustrations and numerous photographs of lamps primarily from England and the continent. It also offers a perspective which enlarges the concept of kerosene lighting and indicates the potential to explore its world-wide use.

Perhaps the most obvious characteristics that serve to distinguish North American from foreign lamps are the differences in design and the relative frequency of style changes. Catalogue illustrations confirm that the design of foreign lamps changed little from the 1890's through the 1930's. In the U.S., catalogues from every decade reveal the abandonment of old styles and introduction of kerosene lamps that more closely reflected both changes in fashion and technology.

In addition to catalogue illustrations, this section shows average to very good examples along with many of exceptional merit. Today there is a good possibility that fine examples of lamps exported a century ago will be found in parts of the world remote from their origin.

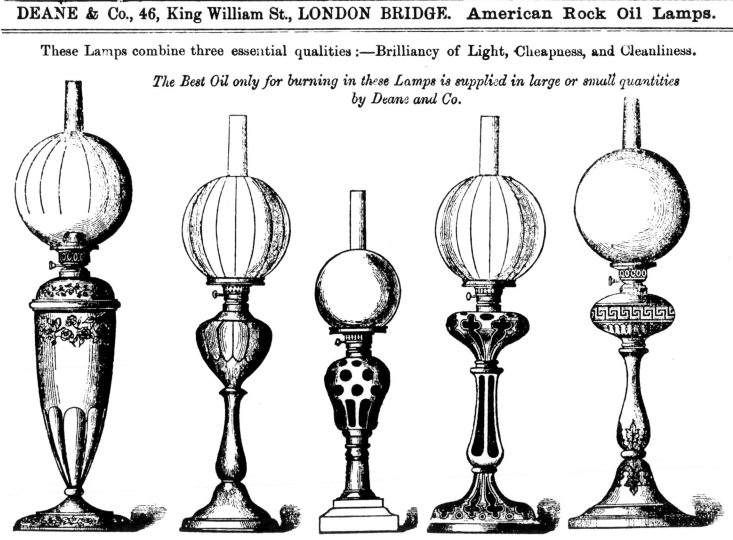

DEANE & Co., 46, King William St., LONDON BRIDGE. American Rock Oil Lamps.

These Lamps combine three essential qualities :—Brilliancy of Light, Cheapness, and Cleanliness.

The Best Oil only for burning in these Lamps is supplied in large or small quantities by Deane and Co.

| Vase Lamp. No. 7—17 in. high to top of Burner, £2 5s. | No. 5—16½ in. high to top of Burner, from 21s. | No. 4—12 in. high to top of burner, fm. 12/6 | No. 6—16½ in. high to top of Burner, from 50s. | No. 8—16 in. high to top of Burner, £1 5s. |

Early catalogue page circa 1860 showing English lamps for burning Rock Oil (kerosene)

Courtesy, Henry Francis du Pont Winterthur Museum Library: Collection of Printed Books

Markings on the combination burner and collar of lamp (a) identify the English burner manufacturer as Hinks & Co. and the American importer as J.H. Covell, 1500 Broadway N.Y. It is a vase lamp in cast and repoussé brass. A frieze of draped putti and grape vines is embossed in thin brass. Probably 1890's, it measures 10-3/4''.

a. Brass vase lamp

The silver presentation lamp (b) bears an 1896 hallmark. The original elaborately engraved inscription, unfortunately damaged by several dents, is repeated in a less detailed manner on the opposite side. It reads:

"Presented
-to-
Louise & Lorne
ON THEIR
SILVER WEDDING
By their affectionate Mother
VICTORIA R.I."

Princess Louise, the daughter of Queen Victoria was the wife of the Marquis of Lorne who served as Governor General of Canada 1878-1883. It is possible that Princess Louise was unable to use it in any of her British residences and may have sent it to Canada for Rideau Hall, the official residence of the Governor General. An uncle of the present owner saved it from being melted down as scrap in Ottawa about 1908.

The silver pillar and base, is filled with composition and weighted. It bears London hallmarks for 1896. A removable cut glass font is combined with an acid-frosted shade decorated with cupids and rococo scrolls. The electroplated brass burner is marked "HINKS & SON / PATENT". The thumbwheel is lettered "MAPPIN & WEBB / LONDON, W. / 158 to 162 / OXFORD ST." Height to the top of the burner is 24-1/2 ''.

b. Silver presentation banquet lamp

Photograph courtesy of the Royal Ontario Museum, Toronto, Canada.

a. Japanese cloisonné lamp signed "A.A. VAN TINE N.Y."

Although the base of lamp (a) is a good example of Japanese cloisonné circa 1900, the balance of the lamp and probably the original design is American. Exotic lamps, designed and made in the U.S., were described in an April 29, 1891 issue of *China Glass and Lamps,* reprinted in OL I p.336. At a time when American-made banquet lamps ranged between three and fifteen dollars, the imported creations sold for hundreds of dollars!

Unfortunately the brass font, burner and shade holder have had a chemical brushed on them, that has removed the original ormolu finish, giving them a uniform dull appearance. The burner thumbwheel is marked "A.A. VAN TINE / 877 BROADWAY N.Y." and the cased and gilt shade is signed "A.A.V. & Co."

Ashley A. Van Tine was apparently the founder of A.A. Van Tine & Co.,[1] a New York firm that specialized in the importation of Orientalia, especially from Japan.[2] Height to the top of the shade is 26-1/2".

For more than a century, the Coalport China Works was one of the largest in the world. Founded in the 1790's, Coalport had contacts with America from its earliest years. The Coalport Company probably made their biggest impact on American taste at the Chicago World's Fair in 1893. Their contribution to the exhibition included the magnificent Queen Elizabeth and Queen Victoria vases, both two feet high and much commented on; a set of dessert plates, each bearing the portrait head of an 18th century beauty, copied from paintings by Gainsborough and Reynolds, and several dinner services decorated with figures in the Court costumes of Louis XVI, together with a variety of other products, including a number of exquisite lamp standards produced especially for the Fair.[3]

The magnificent banquet vase lamp (b), in bone porcelain with overglaze painting and gilding, was made in 1893 for the Columbian Exposition in Chicago. A stand of four pieces bolted together, holds the separate font. The "jewelled" decoration was actually partially cast in the mold, and was painted to simulate pink and red stones with central cabochons of semi-precious "jasper".

Markings include the COALPORT ENGLAND trademark with British Crown and factory founding date, repeated twice in dark green; "BANQUET LAMP / 208306 / Rᴅ" in olive green and "CHICAGO / 1893 / EXHIBITION" in gold. Also painted in gold "V / 339Y", likely the factory coding for the decoration. The green factory trademark is repeated under the font. Height to the top of the collar is 17-1/2".

The Ironbridge Gorge Museum in England has two smaller Coalport lamps on loan. This is the only other example known to them and the only known World's Fair lamp. A number of American firms acted as agents for the Coalport Company during the 19th century. These included M.W. Beveridge of Washington, Bigelow Kennard and Co. of Boston, George Shreve and Co. of San Francisco, and Tiffany and Co. of New York.

When softly illuminated, flowers in the three vases that are an integral part of lamp (c), as well as in the matching pair of vases, would have created a sensational focal point in a late Victorian dining or drawing room. Made by Moore Bros. in England, the signed vases and lamp bear the same 1891 design registration and number "164441". The absence of the name of the country of origin, a customs regulation after 1891, and the brief existence of this company, indicate 1891 was the date of manufacture. Additional markings include number "725" painted in brown on the base of the lamp, probably the artist's number. One of the vases is impressed "MOORE / 2 / 644 / RD."

Lamp and vases are bone porcelain having sculptured leaves, orchids and buds with overglaze enameling and gilding.

Silicon ware, introduced in 1880, was a type of stoneware that was made in a variety of colors and finishes and could be decorated in a number of ways.[1] The Doulton silicon stoneware lamp (d) was made in Lambeth circa 1885.[2] According to author Desmond Eyels, Doulton by 1893 was possibly the largest producer of china and earthware lamps in England.

Similar to Doulton silicon wares circa 1890, the putty-colored vase lamp (e) has a floral decoration on bands of roughened texture. The acid-frosted blown shade is appropriate and probably original. Base marks on the vase include the impressed numbers "118 ⊣", perhaps indicating the model or shape; and "1166" in black ink.

A cast-iron weight in the base is impressed "J. HINKS & SON LIMITED 2451". Height to the top of shade is 20-1/2".

b. Coalport banquet vase lamp

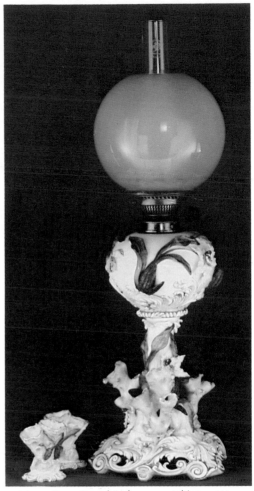

c. Moore Bros. Porcelain lamp; matching vases

d. Doulton Owl lamp
Courtesy, Royal Doulton Tableware Ltd.

e. Doulton-type vase lamp

James Hinks & Son

Most of the better quality English lamps found in North America today have burners and collars made by James Hinks & Son, Limited, Birmingham and London. Their Duplex burners are usually stamped HINKS & SON PATENT between the wick openings; and the collars are often signed.

Hinks burners were used by other manufacturers of lamps in England and on the continent. If the name on the thumbwheel is other than Hinks, it is probably the name of the company that made the other parts, and assembled and sold the complete lamp.

None of the lamps illustrated has a matching shade. It appears that a limited number of shade patterns served to complete all of the lamps. The shades were not included in the price of the lamps, so that combinations found today are not significant.

Although the variety of lamps shown here would appear to accommodate every taste, the styles are decidedly different from those illustrated in American catalogues of the same period. The relatively few pottery lamps that were made in the United States were usually vase lamps with metal fonts.

JAMES HINKS & SON, Limited, Birmingham and London.

a.

JAMES HINKS & SON, Limited, Birmingham and London.

b.

JAMES HINKS & SON, Limited, Birmingham and London.

c.

Courtesy, The Corning Museum of Glass, Corning, New York.

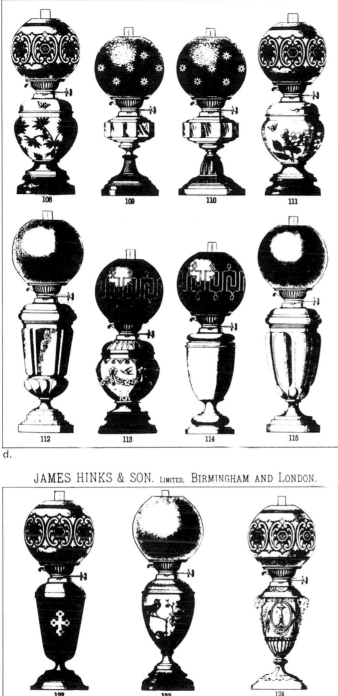

d.

e.

f.

g.

Courtesy, The Corning Museum of Glass, Corning, New York.

a. Hard-paste porcelain lamp with polychrome enamel decoration. Made by G.C. Schierholz & Son, Plaue-on-Havel, Thuringia, Germany about 1880-1900. Height to top of the collar is 6-7/8''.

b. Pottery vase lamp attributed by the owner to W. Zsolnay in Pecs, Hungary. Font is clear glass. The collar is stamped MESSENGER'S PATENT and the thumbwheel marked A.L.C. / DUPLEX / A1. 14'' to top of burner.

c. Opaque pink glass vase lamp with festooned floral polychrome enamel decoration. Probably English: 1880's. Height to top of the collar is 12''.

d. Tin glazed pottery lamp with figural handles, attributed to Germany by the owner. The marked Hinks burner is inscribed No. 2 / HINKS / LEVER on the thumbwheel. Height: 17'' to top of burner.

e. Cast brass mounts and tripod base, surround and support a patterned glass font. The base is alabaster. Continental, probably 1860's. Height: approximately 10'' to top of collar.

f. Fine quality cast-bronze lamp with Sphinx: probably 1860's. The tripod base with monopedia feet is mounted on a marble plinth. Height to top of collar: approximately 11''.

g. Sèvres banquet vase lamp

Lamp; hard paste porcelain with gilt metal handles and mounts. French; bears the marks of the Sèvres Factory, circa 1891-1900. The green ground color is said to have been Napoleon's favorite color from Sèvres.

Such commemorative pieces, complete with portraits and appropriate crests as on the shade, were popular from the late 19th century onward; particularly for fancy decorator vases.

The shade is marked "PHOENIX, MADE EXPRESSLY FOR BURLEY & CO." The Phoenix Glass Company in Monaca, PA near Pittsburgh, was noted for its fine quality hand-painted shades. Height to the top of the shade is 34".

Banquet, Figural and Vase Lamps of the 1880's.   *Courtesy, The Corning Museum of Glass, Corning, New York.*

Silber & Fleming 1879

All with wind-up burners.

No. 670. Moulded Clear Flint Hand Lamp, mounted with ⅝-inch American hinge burner.
The same in blue, green, violet, or amber glass.

No. 667. Hand Lamp, in opal, white, blue, or green crystal glass, mounted with ⅝-inch Comet burner.
The same in new blue, new green, or new royal Bohemian glass.

No. 662. Moulded Crystal Hand Lamp, mounted with ⅞-inch American hinge burner.
The same in turquoise, blue, or chrysoprase green.

No. 608. Moulded Clear Flint Hand Lamp, mounted with ⅝-inch American hinge burner.
The same in blue, green, violet, or amber glass.

No. 782. Bronzed and Relieved Wind-proof Hand Lamp. Price from 6/9 each, including shade. Back or Wall Lamps of similar construction at same prices.

Silber & Fleming were manufacturers, importers and agents with establishments in both London and Paris.

Feldheim, Gotthelf & Co 1905 (Merchants)

No. C 627. Coloured Glass Hand Lamps. Assorted shapes and colours.

No. C 628. White Glass Hand Lamps. Assorted shapes.

No. C 629. Decorated Glass Hand Lamps, with E Venus Burners. Assorted patterns.

No. C 630. White Cut Glass Hand Lamps. Assorted shapes.

No. C 631. Assorted Opal Colour Hand Lamps, with E Venus Burners.

Feldheim, Gotthelf & Co. was a large importer in Sydney, Australia.

Falk, Stadelmann & Co 1933

Extra Large P 8248
Clear Optic, 5-in. diam., with 1-in. Star Burner. 42/0 per doz.

P 8118
Optic Colours, in assorted shapes, 4-in. diam. With Gem Burner,

P 8412
Painted Opal, large 4½-in. size, assorted shapes and decorations, with ¾-in. Star Burner.

P 8507
Rosaline or Ivory Opal, assorted patterns, with ¾-in. Star Burner,

Falk, Stadelmann & Co. were English manufacturers who made the famous 'Veritas' lamps. In the 1930's they offered lamps that had changed little in appearance from those in the 1880's.

Catalogue illustrations and information from *Oil & Kerosene Lamps in Australia* by Peter Cuffley. Courtesy of the author.

a. English lamp by John Walsh Walsh, Soho & Vesta Glass Works, Birmingham, circa 1883-85.[1] Cased clear and pink layers over white. Clear applied icicle fringe and feet. Height to top of burner 9-1/2''.

b. Blown lamp with transfer-printed ''textile'' pattern around stem, over-painted pale yellow. Printed and over-painted floral design on font and foot. Gilt bands. English or Bohemian 1880-1900. Approx. 9''.

c. Blown and cut lamp with clear font and alabaster base. Cutting with broad flat planes is typical of English and Continental lamps. English collar with adapter for American thread. Height is approximately 10-1/2''.

d. Blue alabaster lamp with blown font and base. Good quality with enamelled decoration. Similar recently-made examples have large bubbles and often tin collars. Approx. 11''.

e. Opalescent pink and white lamp with fine diamond-grid optic molding. Painted polychrome floral design with gilt bands and black line trim. Height is approximately 10''.

f. DIETZ & CO. LONDON is embossed on the underside of the base of this lamp. Ruby-stained font with gilt decoration. This lamp resembles American lamps c.1870. Height: 8-1/2''.

Pink centerpiece vase lamp. Striped satin glass with early chimney, probably original.
Rare and unusual form. Bowl approximately 9'' wide

No. 614. Finely decorated Bohemian Glass Vase Lamp, with gilt lines and broad bands in rose, blue, or black, on white ground.

A variety of Bohemian Glass Vase Lamps, finely decorated with flowers, and with flowers and birds, 14 inches high to top of burner, 7/6, 8/9, 9/6, and 10/6 each.

As above, 16 inches high, 12/6, 13/3, 14/9, and 15/6 each.

A large assortment of similar lamps in assorted colours, but without decoration, 12, 14, 15, and 17 inches, prices varying according to size, 5/6, 6/6, 7/6, 8/6, 9/6, and 10/6 each.

No. 355. Vase Table Lamp, decorated with raised flying bird, festoons of flowers, butterflies, and gold lines, movable oil container in white, royal blue, black, celadon, and yellow. In three sizes. Heights to tops of cones, 14¼, 16¼, and 18¼ inches.

No. 355 is a very attractive and saleable lamp, and commands great sale in the colonies, as well as for home trade. Can be had in three sizes, and assorted colours, from 9/6 to 19/6 each.

A similarly decorated lamp, but of different shape and of equal value, at same prices (No. 333 in General Lamp Catalogue).

A variety of upwards of 50 other designs at similar prices.

These lamps are especially suitable for Storm or Punkah Burners.

No. 753. Richly decorated cut crystal enamel Vase Lamp, very handsome, movable oil container.

No. 753 represents a very tasteful description of Crystal Enamel Vase Lamp, of which we have a choice variety in stock, at prices varying from 14/6 to 25/ each, according to size and quality of decoration.

This lamp is at present in great demand, and is very suitable for drawing-room and other purposes.

The above lamps are priced without glass, and with Silber's Patent Circular Burners. They can be had fitted with Silber's Miratus Flat-wick burner at 6d. each less, with Silber's Miratus Duplex burner at 6d. each more, or with ordinary Duplex burner at 1/3 each less.
Most of the above can be had fitted with Storm or Punkah burners at 3/ each extra.

Vase Lamps can be used for Flowers by removing the Oil Container.

Catalogue illustrations courtesy Peter Cuffley

Feldheim, Gotthelf & Co (Merchants) 1905

White Glass Table Lamps,
with Fancy Iron Stands.
A and B Collars. Various shapes.

Decorated Glass Table Lamps, with Fancy Iron Stands and
Duplex Burners. Various patterns.

Decorated Glass Table
Lamps, on Black Base.
Various shapes and sizes.

The sustained market for English lamp styles is pointed out by the tapered example in the centre of the page opposite. It is very similar to one offered by Deane & Co. about twenty years earlier (p. 126). Although Silber & Fleming claimed this lamp commanded great sales in the Colonies, there is little known about the nineteenth-century use of such lamps in Canada. Few foreign lamps have been accepted as part of North America's past, and yet many of those photographed and included in this section were used in nineteenth-century United States and Canada. The note at the bottom of the catalogue page confirms the dual purpose of some vase lamps.

The pronounced flare of the iron bases above gives them a triangular profile. This is a characteristic that immediately distinguishes them from their North American counterparts. A study of contemporary American catalogues also reveals differences in the design of the fonts.

"Bismark" lamps were undoubtedly named after the Prussian statesman. Another variation called Bismark, is shown in a Kiesaw & Co. catalogue, on p. 121 of Cuffley's book. A lamp with the same font as the undecorated Bismark on the right, was advertised in the 1904 Liverpool Lamp & Hardware Co. catalogue.[1]

"Bismarck" Table Lamps.

Decorated "Bismarck" Table Lamps.

Catalogue illustrations courtesy Peter Cuffley.

a. & b. Pair of mold-blown vase lamps.

c. Enamelled vase lamp

d. English vase lamp

a. & b. Pair of good quality English or Continental mold-blown vase lamps. They are opaque white glass with feet applied to the vase parts. Both rims are ground. The exterior of the lamps and shades is enamelled pale matt beige.

The vases have transfer-printed polychrome roundels showing children in the roles of 18th century lovers. Shades are finely painted in polychrome with flower and fruit festoons, birds and nests. American burners and shade holders from the early 1860's appear to be original. Height to the top of the shade, 22-1/2''.

c. A less-tapered mold-blown putty and cream colored vase lamp. The painted white enamel decoration is an inexpensive imitation of the English cameo glass, opposite. Although frequently called ''Mary Gregory'' glass, such pieces usually turn out to be Bohemian.

Painted under the font is ''5'' in dark red. Circa 1880-1900. Height: 12-3/4''.

d. Turquoise-blue vase lamp circa 1890. This example is typical of the better quality English glass lamps.

The two lamps below, *(e)* & *(f)* from the collection of Dr. and Mrs. Leonard S. Rakow, were part of the cameo glass exhibition held at The Corning Museum of Glass in 1982. They were catalogued as follows:

e. England Stourbridge, about 1880,
    probably Thomas Webb & Sons

    Opaque white over frosted colorless on flashed red glass; acid-dipped and cameo-carved.

    Overall floral and geometric patterns, chimney of colorless glass with interior frosted red flashing. Silver collar stamped ''HINKS & SON'S / PATENT''; wick holder stamped ''Hinks & Son Patent''; opaque white glass inset on handle impressed ''HINKS'S / DUPLEX / PATENT.'' Height 20''.

f. England, Wordsley, about 1885,
    probably Stevens & Williams

    Opaque white over frosted light blue on opaque white glass; acid-dipped and cameo-carved.

    Miniature lamp with daisy-like flower on body, white trumpet flowers on shade and a clear glass chimney. Three frosted colorless feet. Brass burner, handle stamped ''Albion Lamp C.º • Birmingham •.''

    Similar lamps appear in the Stevens & Williams design and price books. Height 8''.

e. & f. English cameo lamps
Photograph courtesy The Corning Museum of Glass, Corning, New York
Permission of the owners, Dr. & Mrs. Leonard S. Rakow

g. Blue cameo lamp, circa 1885-90, Probably Thomas Webb & Sons. Hinks & Son burner and collar combination. Height to top of shade 18''

Although English glass companies are reputed to have made relatively large numbers of cameo lamps, few are known to exist today. The standard price of these lamps at the time of manufacture ranged between £100 and £200, depending on size and quality of workmanship.[1] Ray Grover, co-author of *English Cameo Glass,* advised me that he has seen only a handful of complete full-size cameo lamps.

LAMPES A PIED
RÉCIPIENTS

Tarification page 8

E. 164

E. 165

E. 166

E. 167

E. 162

E. 163

E. 168

E. 169

E. 170

E. 171 Décor Or

Consultez observations
générales en tête de l'Album.

— 10 —

Les articles sont reproduits
au quart de leur grandeur naturelle.

Courtesy, The Corning Museum of Glass, Corning, New York.

These lamps, manufactured by the famous Baccarat Company in France, are the exception to the rule that the overall appearance of foreign lamps is distinctly different from those made in America.

The banquet lamps in the above illustration, taken from a 1916 Baccarat Company catalogue, and those advertised by the Fostoria Glass Company in 1906 (see p. 94), appear to be almost identical. Comparison of actual examples may be necessary to identify unmarked lamps.

Falk, Stadelmann & Co 1933

Polished brass on black base, painted opal fount.

Polished brass, on black base. Imitation cut fount.

Polished brass on black base Buff coloured, orange decorated fount.

Polished brass on black base, with green or roseline cut fount.

Polished brass cut crystal fount.

Polished brass, rose or green shaded, decorated fount.

Polished brass. Height 18½ in.

Polished brass with superior decorated fount.

Many lamps similar to the 1933 examples illustrated above, have been imported in recent years, and have been attributed to the nineteenth century. Their design and good quality belies their age, particularly when they are compared with kerosene lamps made in America during the 1930's.

Catalogue illustrations courtesy Peter Cuffley.

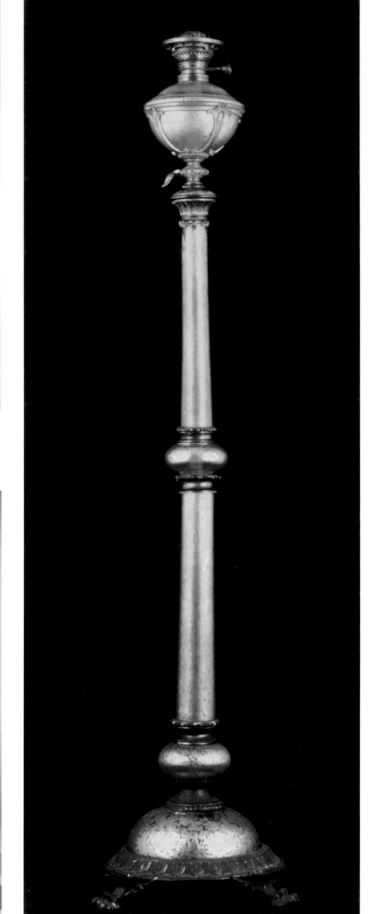

a. English lamp circa 1865. Cased and cut, blue to white to clear with gilt decoration. Shown in the Dietz catalogue in red, green and blue. The shade is probably original.

b. Banquet lamp in clear glass with ruby stain. English — 1890's. English buildings including the Crystal Palace are acid-etched on the frosted shade.

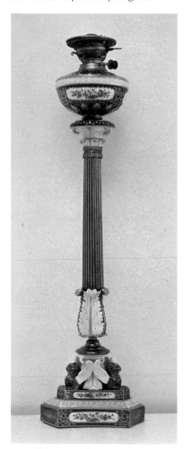

c. Tall banquet lamp in hard-paste porcelain. See opposite page for additional information.

d. English banquet lamp. See catalogue illustration and description opposite.
Courtesy Henry Ford Museum

e. Adjustable floor lamp. Spotted iridescent glass with fine cast-bronze mounts, circa 1900. The glass is Bohemian, Loetz type; American B&H burner.

c. Banquet lamp, probably French 1855-60. The deep-green ground with gilding and floral reserves like a tableware pattern, the thinly glazed white moldings and winged lions, and the simple non-screw attachment between shade and font, all point to a Third Empire date. The pedestal and column are composed of four pieces put together with brass mounts.

This is the kind of lamp that French manufacturers featured at international expositions. The English patented Evered's burner and collar would have been added later. Height to the top of the burner is 34''.

d. This exceptionally-fine lamp was sold by Thomas Rowatt & Sons, a prominent English manufacturer. Like J. Hinks & Son, they patented and manufactured burners, as well as offering complete lamps for sale. The glass, pottery and perhaps other components they used were made elsewhere.

Geometric-cut stem and base and the floral design on the font, are embellished with gilt tracery and metal mounts, set on marble. The 1880 catalogue illustration below, (fig. 1), shows the ball shade that would have been sold with this particular lamp.

Courtesy, Early Auction Company

fig. 1   f.

g. A richly-gilded English vase lamp in deep ruby glass. Matching mold-blown chimney with spiralled pattern. Probably 1880's.

f. Sold at a Phillips (England) auction in 1976, this lamp was catalogued as follows: "A VERY RARE AND COMPLETE RICHARDSON FIVE-COLOUR OIL LAMP, chimney and shade, the lamp and chimney in opaque white striped and festooned in red and yellow, decorated with red raspberry prunts on two knops and with dark blue pincered collar, on wide domed foot festooned in red and bordered in white, the clear glass shade with festooning in opaque white, trailing and bordering in two shades of red, 25'' *overall height*".

Phillips also noted that: "This lamp was purchased from the granddaughter of a Richardson workman—it was made jointly by Joseph Locke and several other glass-blowers as a wedding present for a fellow-worker. It is most unusual for the chimney to be decorated in this way"

A color photograph of this lamp is shown in *The Hallmarks of Antique Glass* by R. Wilkinson.

A FEW SPECIMENS OF

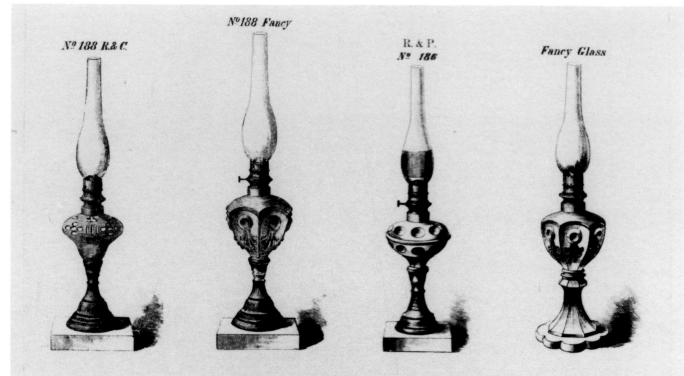

The 1856 Starr, Fellows & Co.'s Pictorial Catalogue of Lamps, Gas Fixtures, &C. stated that: "Our experience in manufacturing covers a period of about 15 years, the first 10 of which were confined exclusively to Lamps and, to those principally of Lamps to burn Camphene and Fluid." In 1850 they added gas fixtures to the line.

A circular dated March 2nd, 1857 noted the name of the company was changed to Fellows, Hoffman & Co. Pages dated 1858, and others dated 1858-1859 with the new name, appear to be supplemental to the earlier catalogue. The undated pages shown here, have the same typeface heading as these later pages, and are the only ones that advertise coal oil. They are the earliest known manufacturer's catalogue illustrations of coal oil or kerosene lamps.

Courtesy, Old Sturbridge Village, Sturbridge, Massachusetts

FELLOWS, HOFFMAN & Co.'s COAL OIL LAMPS.

Salesroom, 71 BEEKMAN STREET, N. Y.

Many of the lamps and fixtures in the 1856 catalogue have component parts that are the same as those found on several kerosene lamps illustrated in the Composite Lamps section, (pp. 45-94), and in both the Dietz and the Russell and Erwin catalogues.

Fellows, Hoffman & Co. would have converted some of their metal pre-kerosene lamps for use with kerosene. Glass lamps simply had a kerosene burner added. The pattern they called R & P is the one I called Ring Punty in OL I, suspecting it to be the same one frequently referred to in the S.A. Southlands catalogue.

The chimneys, shades, burners, fonts, stems and bases illustrated here offer valuable information about the earliest kerosene lamps.

Courtesy, Old Sturbridge Village, Sturbridge, Massachusetts

Russell and Erwin Catalogue

There are two catalogues of exceptional value that record kerosene lamps of the 1860's. One is the Illustrated 1865 Catalogue of American Hardware of the Russell and Erwin Manufacturing Company, New Britain, Connecticut. This catalogue, reprinted by The Association for Preservation Technology, includes not only hardware but many household articles as well.

The second catalogue is the recently reprinted Dietz & Company catalogue, (see Bibliography). Although it is presented as an 1860 Dietz catalogue, the inclusion of articles patented in 1864 indicates circa 1865 would be more accurate. Some portions may have been part of an earlier catalogue; and some of the Russell and Erwin lamps could also have been made before 1865.

Although the lamps illustrated in these selected pages are probably American, many others shown in the Russell and Erwin catalogue and in the Dietz catalogue, appear to have been imported.

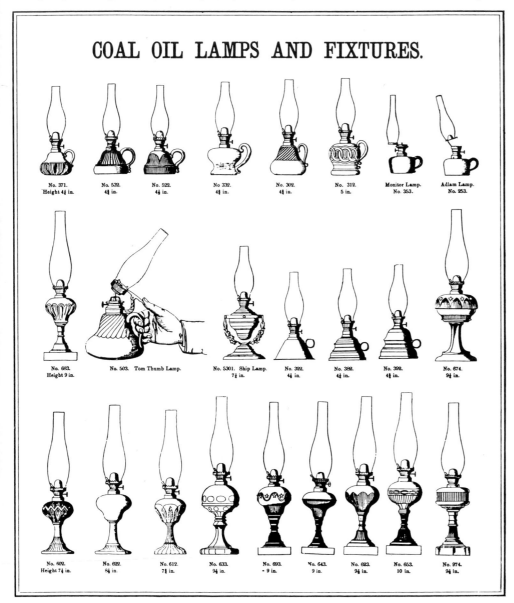

COAL OIL LAMPS AND FIXTURES.

No. 371. Height 4¼ in. — No. 532. 4½ in. — No. 522. 4½ in. — No 332. 4½ in. — No. 302. 4½ in. — No. 312. 5 in. — Monitor Lamp. No. 353. — Adlam Lamp. No. 253.

No. 683. Height 9 in. — No. 503. Tom Thumb Lamp. — No. 5301. Ship Lamp. 7½ in. — No. 392. 4½ in. — No. 382. 4½ in. — No. 392. 4½ in. — No. 674. 9¼ in.

No. 602. Height 7½ in. — No. 622. 8¼ in. — No. 612. 7½ in. — No. 633. 9¼ in. — No. 693. - 9 in. — No. 643. 9 in. — No. 623. 9¼ in. — No. 653. 10 in. — No. 974. 9¼ in.

TOP ROW

No. 371. Similar to others of this period, however I have not seen one that appears to be exactly like this example.

No. 532. See p. 98 d.

No. 522. Two examples of this lamp (see p. 98 e) have been seen. Both apparently had original use in Ontario.

No. 332. This plain lamp is not familiar to me. It would have been an inexpensive utilitarian lamp.

No. 302. See OL 1 p. 88 b. No. 503, Tom Thumb Lamp below, appears to be the same design with patented burner known as Tom Thumb, who of course was Barnum & Bailey's famous midget.

No. 312. Wedding Ring. See p. 54 and OL I p. 166 for mold-blown and pressed, hand and stand lamp examples.

No. 353 and 253. These simple lamps have a familiar shape. The names Monitor and Adlam refer to the patented burners.

MIDDLE ROW

No. 683. California.[ON] See p. 28 and OL I pp. 136, 141 & 153 for the same lamp I described as Atterbury Loop.

No. 503. Tom Thumb Lamp. See No. 302 above.

No. 5301. Ship Lamp. These lamps on gimbals were also used on trains.

No. 322, No. 382 and No. 392. Similar tin and brass lamps continued to be made for about 50 years.

No. 674. Stars and Spears. Clearly a bracket or hanging-lamp font combined with the stem shown on p. 100 b and in OL I p. 117 g & h.

BOTTOM ROW

No. 602. Reed[ON] or Atterbury Double Icicle. See p. 28 and OLI p. 91.

No. 622. Plain font with base that has too little detail to identify.

No. 612. I have not seen an example of this particular font. The base is somewhat suggestive of the Eaton[ON] lamps, on a smaller scale.

No. 633. Concave,[ON] R & P[ON] or Ring Punty. Many examples are illustrated in this book and in OL I.

No. 693. Stars Entwined. See p. 70.

No. 643. Bond. See OL I p. 90.

No. 623. I cannot identify this one.

No. 653. Diamond Band and Half Rib. Similar to ones illustrated in this book and OL I.

No. 974. Grant[ON] or Rand Rib. Several examples of this common font are illustrated in this book and in OL I.

These pages, from the Russell and Erwin 1865 Catalogue are reprinted here through the kind permission of the publishers, The Association for Preservation Technology (see Bibliography).

No.	Size of Burner.	Description.
371	No. 0,	Flint Glass
532	No. 0,	Flint Glass
522	No. 0,	Flint Glass
332	No. 0,	Flint Glass
302	No. 0,	Flint Glass
312	No. 0,	Flint Glass
353	—	Flint Glass, Round Wick, Monitor Burner
253	—	Flint Glass, Adlam Lamp
683	No. 1,	Marble Base, Brass Column, Flint Font, A, B, C and D
503	—	Flint Glass, Round Wick, Tom Thumb Burner.
5301	No. 1,	Brass, Double Swing Ship Lamp
322	No. 0,	Tin, Bronzed
382	No. 0,	Brass, Omula and Bronzed

No.	Size of Burner.	Description.
392	No. 0,	Brass, Omula and Bronzed
674	No. 1,	Flint Glass
602	No. 1,	Flint Glass, A, B, C and D
622	No. 1,	Flint Glass
612	No. 1,	Flint Glass
633	No. 1,	Flint Glass
693	No. 1,	Marble Base, Brass Column, Flint Font, A, B, C and D
643	No. 1,	Marble Base, Brass Column, Flint Font, A, B, C and D
623	No. 1,	Marble Base, Brass Column, Flint Font, A, B, C and D
653	No. 1,	Marble Base, Brass Column, Flint Font, A, B, C and D
974	No. 1,	Alabaster Stand, Flint Font

COAL OIL LAMPS AND FIXTURES.

(Continued.)

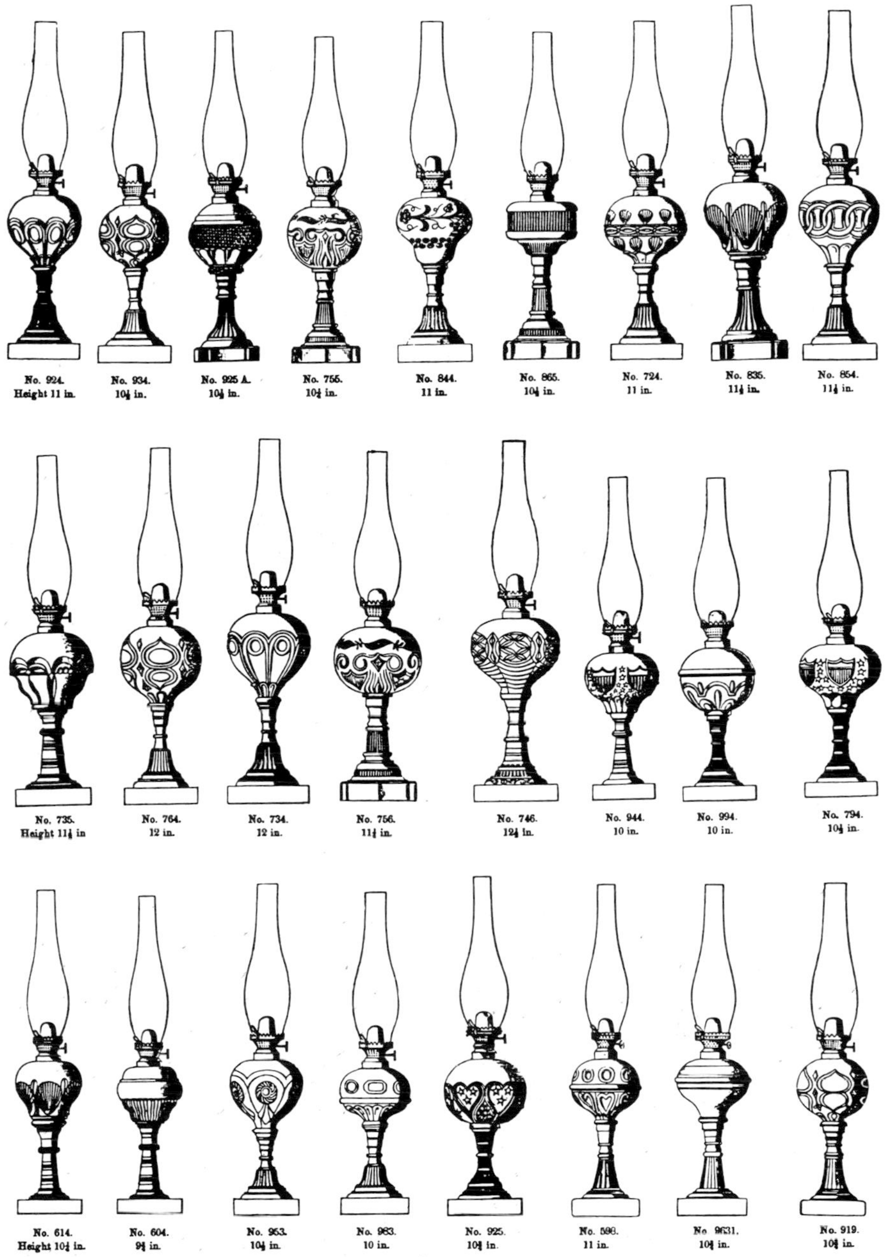
No. 924. Height 11 in.
No. 934. 10¼ in.
No. 925 A. 10½ in.
No. 755. 10½ in.
No. 844. 11 in.
No. 865. 10¼ in.
No. 724. 11 in.
No. 835. 11¼ in.
No. 854. 11¼ in.
No. 735. Height 11¼ in
No. 764. 12 in.
No. 734. 12 in.
No. 756. 11½ in.
No. 746. 12¼ in.
No. 944. 10 in.
No. 994. 10 in.
No. 794. 10¼ in.
No. 614. Height 10½ in.
No. 604. 9¾ in.
No. 953. 10¼ in.
No. 983. 10 in.
No. 925. 10¾ in.
No. 598. 11 in.
No 9631. 10¾ in.
No. 919. 10¾ in.

No.	Size of Burner.	Description.
924	No. 1,	Marble Base, Brass Column, Flint Font.......
934	No. 1,	Marble Base, Brass Column, Flint Font.......
925 A	No. 1,	Opal Base, Brass Column, Flint Font.........
755	No. 1,	Opal Stand, Engraved Font.................
844	No. 1,	Marble Base, Brass Column, Engraved Font...
865	No. 1,	Opal Stand, Brass Column, Flint Font........
724	No. 1,	Marble Base, Brass Column, Flint Font.......
835	No. 1,	Opal Stand, Flint Font.....................
854	No. 1,	Marble Base, Brass Column, Flint Font.......
735	No. 1,	Marble Base, Brass Column, Flint Font.......
764	No. 1,	Marble Base, Brass Column, Flint Font.......
734	No. 1,	Marble Base, Brass Column, Flint Font.......
756	No. 1,	Opal Stand, Engraved Font.................
746	No. 1,	Marble Base, Brass Column, Flint Font.......
944	No. 1,	Marble Base, Brass Column, Flint Font.......
994	No. 1,	Marble Base, Brass Column, Flint Font.......
794	No. 1,	Marble Base, Brass Column, Flint Font.......
614	No. 1,	Marble Base, Brass Column, Flint Font, A, B, C and D................................
604	No. 1,	Marble Base, Brass Column, Flint Font, A, B, C and D................................
953	No. 1,	Marble Base, Brass Column, Flint Font.......
983	No. 1,	Marble Base, Brass Column, Flint Font.......
925	No. 1,	Marble Base, Brass Column, Flint Font.......
598	No. 1,	Alabaster, Gilt Stand, Flint Font, Gilt Band, **Assorted Colors**......................
9631	No. 1,	Alabaster, Gilt Stand, Gilt Font, **Assorted Colors**...............................
919	No. 1,	Alabaster, Gilt Stand, Gilt Flint Font..........

TOP ROW

No. 924. Panelled Bullseye. One of the most common patterns of the 1860's, made at several factories in the East and Midwest. See p. 68 f, 85 n and 106 f as well as examples in OL I.

No. 934. Flame Bullseye, closely resembles Excelsior patterns. A common pressed pattern, usually of excellent quality. Examples in the Related Lamps section and in OL I.

No. 925A. Sawtooth Band and Panel. See OL I p. 170. Both excellent pressed quality and average quality mold-blown examples have been seen.

No. 755. Owl and Shield. See OL I p. 117. Scroll and Shield would be a more appropriate name.

No. 844. I have not seen an engraved or cut font exactly like this one.

No. 865. Grant.ON Same font as No. 974, p. 148, combined with a slightly different base.

No. 724. Diamond Band and Fan. See p. 63 f.

No. 835. Shell and Dart. See p. 63 i.

No. 854. Wedding Ring. See p. 148 top row.

MIDDLE ROW

No. 735. Heart-top Panel. See pp. 32 & 37 and OL I p. 167.

No. 764. Flame Bullseye. See No. 934 above.

No. 734. Panelled Bullseye. See No. 924 above.

No. 756. Owl and Shield. See No. 755 above.

No. 746 Triple Diamond Medallion. See p. 84 and OL I p. 160.

No. 944. Shield and Star. See p. 98 and OL I p. 105.

No. 994. Punctuated Loop. See p. 74.

No. 794. Shield and Star. See No. 944.

BOTTOM ROW

No. 614. Shell and Dart. See No. 835 top row.

No. 604. Tapered Rib. See pp. 71 & 98.

No. 953. Feathered Bullseye and Fleur-de-lis. See p. 110.

No. 983. Ring Punty and Oval. This is a Ring Punty variation that I have not seen.

No. 925. Hearts and Stars. See pp. 41-42 and OL I, pp. 124, 125 & 145.

No. 598. Ring Punty and Heart. See OL I p. 86.

No. 9631. Simple unidentified font.

No. 919. Flame Bullseye. See No. 934 above.

COAL OIL LAMPS AND FIXTURES.

(Continued.)

No. 9401. Height 10¼ in. No. 7802. 10½ in. No. 7321. 12 in. No. 5441. 11¼ in. No. 1171. 12¼ in. No. 859. 11¼ in. No. 9741. 11 in. No. 7932. 11¼ in.

No. 4921 Height 10¼ in. No. 9612. 11¼ in. No. 907. 12¼ in. No. 917. 13 in. No. 927. 13 in. No. 796. 12¼ in. No. 996. 13¼ in.

No. 1161. Height 13¼ in. No. 528. 12¼ in. No. 9711. 13¼ in. No. 749. 13¼ in. No. 8991. 14¼ in. No. 8341. 13 in.

No.	Size of Burner.	Description.
9401	No. 1,	Alabaster, Gilt Stand, Flint Font, Gilt Band...
7802	No. 1,	Alabaster, Gilt Stand, Opal, Gilt and Painted Font.
7321	No. 1,	Alabaster, Gilt Stand, Gilt Flint Font.
5441	No. 1,	Alabaster, Gilt Stand, Gilt Font, **Assorted Colors**.
1171	No. 1,	Marble Base, Bronze Figure, Gilt Font, **Assorted Colors**.
859	No. 1,	Marble Base, Bronze Column, Flint Font.
9741	No. 1,	Alabaster, Gilt Stand, Flint Gilt Font, **Assorted Colors**.
7932	No. 1,	Glass Stand, **Assorted Colors**, Alabaster, Painted and Gilt Font.
4921	No. 1,	Alabaster, Gilt Stand, Flint Gilt Font, **Assorted Colors**.
9612	No. 1,	Alabaster, Gilt Stand, Flint Gilt Font.
907	No. 1,	Marble, Double Base, Brass Column, Eng'd Font.
917	No. 1,	Marble, Double Base, Brass Column, Flint Font.
927	No. 1,	Marble, Double Base, Brass Column, Flint Font.
796	No. 1,	Marble, Double Base, Brass Column, Flint Font.
996	No. 1,	Marble, Double Base, Brass Column, Flint Font.
1161	No. 2,	Alabaster, Gilt Stand, Flint Gilt Font.
528	No. 2,	Marble Base, Brass Column, Flint Font.
9711	No. 2,	Marble, Double Base, Bronze Column, Flint Font
749	No. 2,	Marble Base, Brass Column, Flint Font.
8991	No. 2,	Alabaster Gilt Stand, Flint Gilt Font.
8341	No. 2,	Alabaster Double Base, Gilt Flint Engr'd Font.

TOP ROW

No. 9401. Sawtooth Band and Panel. See No. 925A. Top row, p. 149.

No. 7802. Decorated plain font.

No. 7321. Flame Bullseye. See top row, p. 149.

No. 5441. I have not seen an alabaster gilt font exactly the same as this one. There could be some artist's license here.

No. 1171. Interesting spelter base. The shading at the side of the font indicates there were gilt bands around the widest parts and a gilt design on the shoulder.

No. 859. This drawing was probably intended to illustrate Triple Flute and Bar, or perhaps Triple Flute. Several examples of this well-known pattern are illustrated in the Related Lamps section and in OL I.

No. 9741. Clear font with gilt floral or scroll design on the shoulder as indicated by the shading at the edge of the font. Similar shade holders and shades for stand lamps were popular until about 1880. The shades were also used on student lamps.

No. 7932. Scenic design with mountains painted on the alabaster font.

MIDDLE ROW

No. 4921. A gilt floral or scroll design above the rib is indicated.

No. 9612. Flame Bullseye font. See 7321 top row p. 149.

No. 907. This font, described as engraved, appears to be cased and cut.

No. 917. Triple Diamond Medallion. See No. 746 Middle row, p. 149.

No. 927. Flame Bullseye. See No. 934 top row, p. 149.

No. 796. Wedding Ring. See No. 312 top row, p. 148.

No. 996. Panelled Bullseye. See No. 924 top row, p. 149.

BOTTOM ROW

No. 1161. Sawtooth Band and Panel. See No. 925A top row, p. 149.

No. 528. Owl and Shield. See No. 785 top row, p. 149.

No. 9711. Cottage with Fleur-de-lis. See p. 25 and OL I for other examples.

No. 749. Flame Bullseye. See No. 934 top row, p. 149.

No. 8991. Cottage with Fleur-de-lis. See No. 9711, left.

No. 8341. Owl and Shield. See No. 755 top row, p. 149.

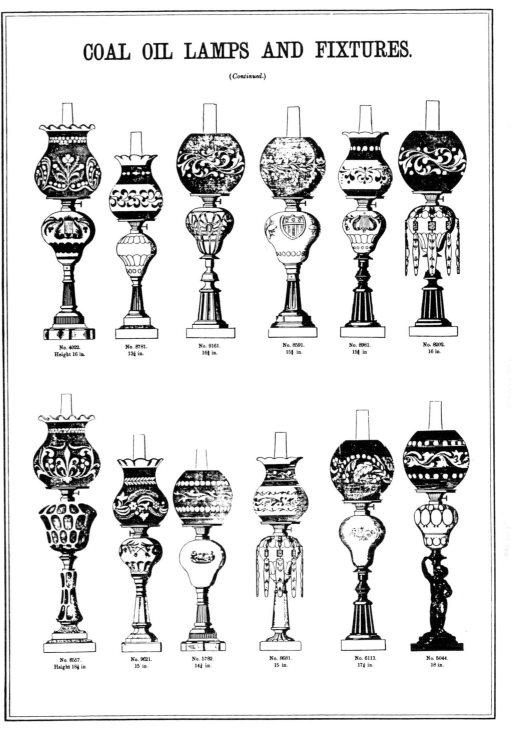

COAL OIL LAMPS AND FIXTURES.

(Continued.)

No. 4022. Height 16 in.	No. 8781. 13¾ in.	No. 9161. 16¼ in.	No. 8591. 15¼ in.	No. 8961. 15¾ in	No. 8202. 16 in.

No. 6557. Height 18¼ in.	No. 9621. 15 in.	No. 5782. 14¼ in.	No. 8681. 15 in.	No. 6113. 17¼ in.	No. 5044. 18 in.

TOP ROW

No. 4022. Cut and engraved lyre font. See p. 80 and OL I p. 108.

No. 8781. On the right hand side of this font, there is an indication that the gilt decoration described is a typical scroll design.

No. 9161. Gothic pattern. See p. 66. The stem and base design of this and other lamps on this page was shown on a lamp advertised in 1847.[1]

No. 8591. The only example of this lamp font that I have seen had a deeply-cut shield with a shallow pattern in between.

No. 8981. See No. 4022, far left.

No. 8202. Apparently the same font as No. 8781 with the addition of a prism ring and prisms, and an earlier base.

BOTTOM ROW

No. 6557. See p. 53 d.

No. 9621. Lyre font. See No. 4022 top row. This view shows the pattern detail on the sides.

No. 5782. Scenic design on font.

No. 8681. Same as 8202 above except for the base and shade.

No. 6113. Roses painted on a plain font.

No. 5044. I have seen two other fonts like this, combined with different bases.

No.	Size of Burner.	Description.
4022	No. 2,	Alabaster Gilt Stand, Fine Engraved Font....
8781	No. 2,	Marble Double Base, Gilt or Bronzed Column, Flint Cut and Gilt Font..................
9161	No. 2,	Marble Base, Gilt or Bronzed Column, Flint Font, A, B and C........................
8591	No. 2,	Opal Double Base, Gilt Fine Cut Flint Font...
8981	No. 2,	Marble Base, Bronze or Gilt Column..........
8202	No. 2,	Marble Base, Bronze or Gilt Column, Flint Cut Font.................................

No.	Size of Burner.	Description.
6557	No. 2,	Marble Base, Rich Plated and Cut **Assorted Colors**.................................
9621	No. 2,	**Alabaster Stand, Fine Cut and Engraved Font.**
5782	No. 2,	Alabaster Gilt Stand, Rich Painted and Gilt Alabaster Font...........................
8681	No. 2,	Marble Base, Glass Column, **Assorted Colors,** Plated and Cut Fonts, **Assorted Colors**..
6113	No. 2,	Marble Base, Bronze or Gilt Column, Opal Gilt Painted Peg...........................
5044	No. 2,	Black Marble Base, Fine Cut Cast Bronze Stand, Fonts Plated and Cut, **Assorted Colors**...

Appendix

fig. 1. Courtesy The Henry Ford Museum Library, Gift of Preston R. Bassett.

The invoice (fig. 1) dated exactly ten months before "Colonel" Edwin L. Drake struck oil in Titusville, PA is additional evidence that the sale of kerosene lamps was established before that momentous historical event. It is also significant from the standpoint of glassmaking because it lists several "Ala" lamps. Initially this was a puzzling description, but as my research progressed it became apparent that "Ala" was an abbreviation for alabaster glass and also that alabaster glass was a type referred to throughout the nineteenth century kerosene period. Although references to alabaster glass are inexplicably inconsistent, the acceptance of the term is indisputable. The following list of primary source material confirms this.

1858
The Boston and Sandwich Glass Company invoice (fig. 1), listing "Ala" (alabaster) lamps.

1865
In the Russell and Erwin catalogue (pp. 148-151) nineteen of the illustrated fonts and bases are described as alabaster.
The Boston & Sandwich Glass Company catalogue illustrates lamps described as both opal and alabaster (OL I p. 107). The known opal examples are opaque white and the alabaster description probably applies to the lamp on p. 52 a.

1868
Handwritten formulas for glass signed "Sandwich Aug. 7th 1868 James G. Lloyd" include two receipts for white alabaster and nine for colored.[1] The following paragraph by Wilson[2] identifies and offers relative information.

"In 1858 Deming Jarves withdrew from the Boston & Sandwich Glass Company, which he had founded in 1825, and along with James D. Lloyd, who had begun work at the Sandwich factory as a young boy and had become a mixer and color expert, organized and founded the Cape Cod Glass Works in Sandwich, Massachusetts. The factory was located only a few blocks from the works of the Boston & Sandwich Glass Company, and probably many of the fragments found by collectors in Sandwich are from the factory, rather than from the original Sandwich works."

Undated notes
An undated notebook containing both notes and formulas was acquired by the Henry Ford Museum from George E.

Burbank, a Sandwich resident for many decades. There are some similarities between these and the Lloyd formulas. Nine "Alabaster Colors" are listed including one for Alabaster white or Pate de Riz. The accompanying notes describe conditions under which the metal can become quite transparent.

1884
A handwritten page with five formulas includes one for "Alabaster Dove" and one for "Alabaster Turquoise."[3] The page is headed "Receipts from G.L. Fessenden, April 29th 1884." George L. Fessenden was related to Sewall H. Fessenden listed as Agent on the invoice (fig. 1).

Union wage agreements record wages and production requirements of alabaster electric lamp globes (shades). They also note that "Alab. 10 per cent less in move than crystal and opal."

1908
Harry Bastow, a Midwest glassmaker who began his career in the nineteenth century, wrote the following description of two types of alabaster.[4]

"In alabaster, there are many so-called alabaster effects which are merely produced by using a reduced quantity of the same materials as used for opal, but smoothness and uniformity of color are practically impossible under these conditions, and the only alabaster worthy of the name is made from entirely different materials and under working conditions which are different. This kind of alabaster shows a uniform semi-opaque color with flake effects showing apparently just under the surface. This alabaster gives particularly beautiful bisque effects when the surface is etched."

Many lamps in English and Continental wholesale catalogues are also described as alabaster.

All of this information confirms that in both Europe and America, alabaster was an accepted term for glass with certain distinctive qualities. It is non-opalescent, more or less granular and has considerable latitude with regard to opacity. It may have whitish flecks and can be white or colored. This description fits thousands of lamps, particularly those made in America before 1880. To call them alabaster would simplify description and communication. It would undoubtedly be more accurate than using the terms opaline, clambroth or clam-water and certainly less confusing. Future research may idenfiy the characteristics of opaline glass and record its history. At the present time however, alabaster is the most appropriate term for lamps.

While there is apparently no evidence to refute alabaster as a valid term there is a curious lack of supportive evidence in certain areas. Alabaster is *not* mentioned in the following price lists or catalogues:
S.E. Southlands Catalogue and wholesale Price List circa 1859 (OL I pp. 18-19).
Cape Cod Glass Company, 1860's (p. 30).
M'Kee & Brothers, four catalogues, 1860's (p.31).
Atterbury & Co. four catalogues 1872-1881.
There are however numerous examples of both Atterbury and Ripley, catalogued and/or patented lamps, that fit the description of alabaster.

The catalogues that do describe alabaster lamps, appear to reserve this description for white alabaster glass, and yet the formulas and lamps extant indicate colored alabaster was a common type of glass. Future research and perhaps experimentation with the formulas should prove enlightening.

Notes

p.9 [1]Much of the information in Glass and Glassmaking was discovered or made available after the first draft was written. The two main sources, *The Scientific American* vol.VIII, no.5 (January 31, 1863) and the writings of Harry Bastow, are so rich in contemporary descriptions that they are excerpted extensively and in a few instances have modified my original text.

The Scientific American in an article entitled ''The Manufacture and Cutting of Flint-Glass'' recorded observations made during a visit to the world-renowned Brooklyn Flint Glass Works. Later moved to Corning, NY it became the Corning Glass Works, still in operation today.

Frank L. Fenton, founder of the Fenton Art Glass Company, was closely associated with Harry Bastow before the turn of the century. The copy of Bastow's book cited is the one Frank M. Fenton inherited from his father.

Harry Bastow, *American Glass Practice: A practical book devoted to actual glass factory conditions, with problems discussed in a manner that will be readily understood by the layman.* (Pittsburgh, Pennsylvania: The Glassworker, 1920).

Harry Bastow, *Decorative Color Effects in Glass* (Glass and Pottery World, April 1908) vol.XVII, no.4, p.32.

Contemporary descriptions are not always infallible but they are the best primary source material available. Direct exposure of this information where it is clearly described and not at variance with other sources, is the most accurate presentation of the terms and technology of the kerosene era.

p.9 [2]From Parker and Delaplaines American edition, New Edinburgh Encyclopedia.

p.10 [1]McKearin and Wilson, *American Bottles and Flasks*, pp.12-14.

p.11 [1]U.S. Patent no.35430 (June 3, 1862).

[2]Other conditions within the glass are sometimes referred to as *cords*; however this does not apply to lamps I have examined.

[3]*Scientific American* vol.VIII, no.5 (January 31, 1863).

p.12 [1]Ibid

[2]During testimony given before the Commissioner of Patents, May 19, 1879, in a matter of interference between the applications of F.S. Shirley, Washington Beck and Frederick Von Hofe, Beck described a feature of his patent: ''These lines should be deep enough so that the particles of sand adhering to the brush would not strike the bottom of the depression.''

p.14 [1]Undated, unsigned notebook in the Ford Museum collection. While undated it appears to be from the third quarter of the nineteenth century. It contains many formulas for cased glass and for alabaster glass, as well as notes relating to the formulas and techniques.

[2]Chairman of the Board, The Fenton Art Glass Company.

[3]Bastow, *Decorative Color Effects in Glass*.

[4]When making large objects the weight and distribution may be more easily controlled if a second gather is obtained after the initial one is blocked.

p.15 [1]Private Collection

[2]Paul Hollister, *Travels in Style: Bohemian-American*, (The Glass Club Bulletin of the Early American Glass Club, Spring/Summer 1982) pp.14-16.

[3]Thuro, *Oil Lamps I* pp.18-19

p.16 [1]Dietz catalogue plate 1, no.1055.

[2]Thuro, *Oil Lamps I* p.107.

p.22 [1]*Asher & Adams' Pictorial Album of American Industry 1876* (New York: Rutledge Books 1976 reprint) p. 49.

p.24 [1]In OL I p. 142 a I called this pattern Ohio and stated it was illustrated in the 1874 Atterbury & Co. catalogue. In all other Atterbury catalogues it is called Sherman, indicating that the names in the 1874 catalogue were transposed.

p.25 [1]Russell and Erwin catalogue page reproduced on p.150, no.859.

[2]Dietz Catalogue, plate 13, no.1008.

p.26 [1]U.S. Patent no.117157 (July 18, 1871).

p.27 [1]In testimony given before the Commissioner of Patents, May 19, 1879 (see p.12).

[2]Winterthur Library Collection.

p.31 [1]Wilson, *New England Glass* pp. 297-298

[2]M'Kee and Brothers, *M'Kee Victorian Glass: Five Complete Glass Catalogs from 1859/60 to 1871* (Corning, New York: The Corning Museum of Glass in association with Dover Publications, Inc., New York).

p.35 [1]Thuro, *Oil Lamps I*, pp. 20, 84-85.

[2]Results of X-Ray diffraction and flame photometer tests conducted by John Gray on a 3 milligram sample taken from the inside of the glass stem, showed the following analysis in order of weight and percentage:

Fe	iron	.12 milligrams	4%
NI	nickel	.025	.83%
Ag	silver	.0035	.12%
Hg	mercury	.00025	.008%

This represents about 5% of the total mass. The balance was material used as binding agents (not minerals).
Because the percentage of silver is much greater than mercury, and because we do not know if that small amount of mercury may have been present in the silver, it would be safe to call it a silvered lamp. All these minerals will amalgamate and it is difficult to know whether at that time (circa 1860) they could purify silver as well as they can now.

[3]Wilson, *New England Glass*, pp.312-314.

p.42 [1]Oglebay Institute library.

[2]U.S. Patent no.161912 (Apr. 13, 1875) and U.S. Patent no.175022 (Mar. 21, 1876).

p.43 [1]Miller, *The New Martinsville Glass Story*
[2]Ibid

p.44 [1]U.S. Patent Office library
[2]Two Eaton brothers, Frederick (1809-1865) and James (1817-1856), as well as James' son William, worked at the Boston & Sandwich factory. These lamps may have been named after this family. (*Information courtesy The Sandwich Glass Museum*).

[3]U.S. Patent no.170219 (Nov. 23, 1875).

p.49 [1]Ronald Olmstead, ''A Solar Lamp Maker Rediscovered,'' The Rushlight, XLIX, no.2 (June 1983), p.18

p.50 [1]Wilson, *New England Glass*, pp.225-228 for examples of Thomas Cains lamps.

p.54 [1]Kenneth M. Wilson Collection.

p.56 [1]Catherine M.V. Thuro, *Victorian Flower Stands* (Toronto: Canadian Collector), January/February 1979, pp.25-28.

p.56 [2]*The Rushlight* vol.XLIII, no.2. (June 1977) pp.2-6. The latticinio technique used involved a mold that held thirty canes of glass, either six colored having four white in between or five colored with five white in between.

p.66 [1]Lee, *E.A.P.G.* p.172, plate 55.

[2]M'Kee and Bros. *M'Kee Victorian Glass*.

[3]Spillman, *American and European Pressed Glass*, p.269.

[4]Revi, *American Pressed Glass and Figure Bottles*, p.252.

p.69 [1]Although the three original settlers of Sandwich, in 1637, named Fish must have left thousands of descendants, none in the 1860 (Sandwich) census had the initials R.F. This lamp could have been made for someone living in a nearby town, or elsewhere. (*Courtesy Sandwich Glass Museum*).

p.70 Russell, pp.178-179

p.80 [1]R.C. Barret, *Bennington Patterns in Porcelain*. Plate 208 and color plate c. This mark was used until 1858.

P.86 [1]Kamm I, p.13

[2]Smithsonian Institution.

p.95 [1]Brilliant Cut Glass Collections in the following American Museums: Corning Museum of Glass, Corning, NY. The Henry Ford Museum, Dearborn, MI. Lightner Museum, St. Augustine, FL. Toledo Museum of Art, Toledo, OH.

p.98 [1]Henry & Nathan Russell & Day 1889 catalog. Smithsonian Institution. This lamp appears to have been popular for a few decades.

p.99 [1]*The American Potter and Illuminator*, vol.7, no.2 (Feb. 1888) p.37.

[2]Metz, *Book 2*, Pattern no.1756, pp.138-139.

[3]Ferson, *Yesterday's Milk Glass* p.163.

[4]Kamm II, p.64.

p.100 [1]Ann Gilbert McDonald, *Lighting Series Part VI: The Lamps of Dithridge and Company* (Dubuque, Iowa: The Antique Trader Annual of Articles, 1982), vol.XIV, pp.247-249.

[2]Ferson, *Yesterday's Milk Glass* p.134

p.101 [1]*The American Potter & Illuminator*, vol.7 no.2 (February 1888) p.37.

[2]Henry & Nathan Russell & Day 1889 Catalogue. Smithsonian.

p.103 [1]Kamm V, plate II

[2]Heacock, *A New Look at Old Pattern Glass* (Dubuque, Iowa: The Antique Trader Weekly) p.85.

[3]Measell, *Greentown Glass*, p.86

[4]Corning Museum library.

[5]Lucas, pp.236, 312-315, 320-323.
A few years ago I became aware of a relatively large number of opaque Heart Lamps in all forms, with bright enamelled decoration. Long-time collectors and dealers that I have consulted had not seen decorated Heart Lamps before about 1975.

p.104 [1]Kamm VII, plates 62-63.

[2]OL I pp.152 & 236. This is the fourth book son Randy has had a hand in.

[3]*Pottery and Glassware Reporter*, vol.19, (Aug. 16, 1888) p.17.

p.106 [1]Kamm IV, p.19

p.107 [1]Barker 1877 design patent no. 9848.

[2]Lucas, pp.104-105.

p.111 [1]*Pottery and Glassware Reporter*, vol.23, (July 31, 1890) p.18.

p.112 [1] Ann Gilbert McDonald, *New Discoveries in Night Lamps Part I* (Dubuque, Iowa: The Antique Trader Annual of Articles, 1981), vol. XIII, pp.8-10

[2] Heacock, Book 3, p.54

p.113 Kamm VI, plate 81.

p.114 [1] *Pottery & Glassware Reporter*, vol.25 (June 11, 1891)

[2] *Ibid* vol.23 (June 12, 1890).

[3] Smith, *Findlay Glass*, p.35.

[4] *Pottery & Glass Reporter*, vol.25 (June 11, 1891).

p.115 [1] *American Potter and Illuminator*, vol.7, no.2. (Feb. 1888) p.37.

p.117 [1] *Ibid* vol.5, no.4 (Apr. 1886). p.34.

p.118 [1] Smith, *Findlay Glass*, p.56

p.119 [1] *Pottery & Glassware Reporter*, vol.21 (July 1889) p.4.

[2] Kamm III, p.5 and Metz 2, pp.134-135, pattern no.1137.

[3] Kamm III, p.57.

p.122 [1] McDonald, *Evolution of the Night Lamp*, p.28. Advertisement reproduction.

This lamp with plain font was named Delaware[ON] and with matching font and triparted stem, Dakota.[ON]

[2] Kamm VI, plate 17

p.123 [1] *American Potter and Illuminator*, vol.7, no.2 (Feb. 1888) pp. 36-37.

[2] Marcella Bond, *The Beauty of Albany Glass*, p.75.

[3] *Ibid* pp.7-8, 18.

[4] This company had branches in several U.S. cities and one in Canada; The Pittsburgh Lamp, Brass and Glass Company of Canada, London, Ontario. The catalogue is a reliable source of information, particularly for vase lamps.

p.124 [1] Bond, *Albany Glass*, p.75

p.125 [1] Corning Museum of Glass library.

p.128 [1] *Trow's New York City Directories 1885-1898* (New York: Trow Directory, Printing & Bookbinding Co.).

[2] *House Beautiful Magazine*, 1911 issues.

China Glass & Lamps, vol.1-20 (1891) p.21.

[3] Information on Coalport China in America was provided by Mark Pemberton, Assistant Curator, Ironbridge Gorge Museum, Shropshire, England.

p.129 [1] Desmond Eyles, *Royal Doulton 1815-1865: The Rise and Expansion of the Royal Doulton Potteries*, (London: Hutchinson of London, 1965) pp.45-46.

[2] *Royal Doulton Review 1978* (London: Doulton & Co. 1979) pp.46-47.

p.136 [1] A rose bowl of similar design appeared in an advertisement of John Walsh Walsh, Soho & Vesta Glass Works, Birmingham, in the *Pottery Gazette*. The advertisement is reproduced by Barbara Morris in *Victorian Table Glass and Ornaments* (London: Barrie and Jenkins, 1978) p.228.

p.139 [1] Winterthur Museum Library – Rare Book Collection.

p.151 [1] Ronald Olmstead, *A Solar Lamp Maker Rediscovered*, The Rushlight, vol.XLIX no.2 (June 1983) p.18.

p.152 [1] Collection, The Henry Ford Museum Library.

[2] Wilson, *New England Glass & Glassmaking*, p.134. Courtesy of the Author.

[3] Collection, The Henry Ford Museum Library

[4] *Glass and Pottery World*, vol.XVI, no.4, p.32.

Addenda

a. Aladdin kerosene lamps from *Aladdin: The Magic Name in Lamps* by J.W. Courter. *Courtesy of the author.*

Aladdin kerosene mantle lamps have been made from 1909 until the present day. They were especially popular in rural homes without electricity. These lamps were made in many different styles and colors in glass and metal. Today they are avidly sought and studied by a large number of collectors.

b. Carlisle 1 & 4

These two lamps, also illustrated in OL I p.263 are shown here to facilitate the identification of this family of lamps (see p.112).

Bibliography

American Historical Catalog Collection. *Lamps and Other Lighting Devices 1850-1906.* Princeton: The Pyne Press, 1972.

———— *Pennsylvania Glassware, 1870-1904* Princeton: The Pyne Press, 1972.

Anthony, Robert T. *19th Century Fairy Lamps.* Manchester, Vermont: Forward's Color Productions, Inc., 1969.

Antique & Colonial Lighting. *Pilabrasgo Success Oil Lamps and Decorated Vases.* Catalogue No. 13. Reprint. Clarence, New York: 1982.

The Association for Preservation Technology. *Illustrated Catalogue of American Hardware of the Russell and Erwin Manufacturing Company.* 1865 Catalogue reprint with an introduction by Lee H. Nelson. Baltimore, Maryland: 1980.

Belknap, E. McCamby. *Milk Glass.* New York: Crown Publishers, 1949.

Bennett, Harold & Judy. *Catalogue of Table Glassware, Lamps, Barware, and Novelties: The Cambridge Glass Company.* 1903 Catalogue reprint. Cambridge, Ohio: Harold & Judy Bennett, 1976.

Blount, Bernice and Henry. *French Cameo Glass.* Des Moines, Iowa: Dr. & Mrs. Henry C. Blount, Jr., 1968.

Bond, Marcelle. *The Beauty of Albany Glass (1893 to 1902).* Berne, Indiana: Publishers Printing House, 1972.

Boyd, Ralph and Louise. *Greentown,* 2nd ed. Lagro, Indiana: Commercial Printing, 1970.

Christensen, Erwin O. *The Index of American Design.* New York: The Macmillan Company, 1950.

Collector Books. *Collector's Illustrated Price Guide to Lamps.* Paducah, Kentucky: 1977.

Collector Books. *Fostoria Glass Company — Full Line Catalogue.* 1901 Catalogue reprint. Paducah, Kentucky.

Corning Museum of Glass, The. *Glass Collections in Museums in the United States and Canada.* Corning, New York: 1982.

Cooke, Lawrence S. *Lighting in America: From Colonial Rushlights to Victorian Chandeliers.* New York: University Books, 1975.

Courter, J.W. *Aladdin The Magic Name in Lamps.* Simpson, Illinois: J.W. Courter, 1971.

J.W. Courter Enterprises. *The Plume and Atwood Manufacturing Company.* Circa 1906 Catalogue reprint. Simpson, Illinois: 1975.

Cuffley, Peter. *Oil & Kerosene Lamps in Australia.* Victoria, Australia: Pioneer Design Studio Pty Ltd., 1982.

Cushion, John P. *Pocket Book of British Ceramic Marks.* 3rd ed. London: Faber and Faber, 1976.

Delmore, Mrs. Edward J. *Victorian Miniature Oil Lamps.* Manchester, Vermont: Forward's Color Productions, Inc., 1968

Dietz, Ulysses G. *Victorian Lighting: The Dietz Catalogue of 1860.* Watkins Glen, New York: American Life Foundation, 1982.

Fairweather Antiques. *Edward Miller & Co. Illustrated Catalogue of Bronzed, Decorated, and Real Bronze Lamps and Cigar Lighters, Meriden, Conn., U.S.A.* 1881 Catalogue reprint. Meriden, Connecticut, 1976.

Fauster, Carl U. *Libbey Glass since 1818: Pictorial History & Collector's Guide.* Toledo, Ohio: Len Beach Press, 1979.

Ferson, Regis F., & Mary F. *Yesterday's Milk Glass Today.* Pittsburgh, Pennsylvania: Regis & Mary Ferson, 1981.

Florence, Gene. *The Collectors Encyclopedia of Depression Glass.* 4th ed. Paducah, Kentucky: Collector Books, 1979.

Freeman, Dr. Larry. *New Light on Old Lamps.* Watkins Glen, New York: Century House, 1968.

Godden, Geoffrey A. *Encyclopaedia of British Pottery and Porcelain Marks.*

Greguire, Helen D. *Carnival in Lights.* Arcade, New York: New Books, 1975.

Grover, Ray and Lee. *English Cameo Glass.* New York: Crown Publishers, Inc., 1980.

Hammond, Dorothy. *Confusing Collectibles.* Des Moines, Iowa: Wallace-Homestead Book Co., 1969.

Hayward, Arthur G. *Colonial and Early American Lighting.* Third edition. New York: Dover Publications Inc., 1962.

Heacock, William. *Encyclopedia of Victorian Colored Pattern Glass Book 1: Toothpick Holders from A to Z.* Jonesville, Michigan: Antiques Publications, 1974.

———— *Encyclopedia of Victorian Colored Pattern Glass Book 2: Opalescent Glass from A to Z.* Jonesville, Michigan: Antique Publications, 1975.

———— *Encyclopedia of Victorian Colored Pattern Glass Book 3: Syrups, Sugar Shakers & Cruets from A to Z.* Jonesville, Michigan: Antique Publications, 1976.

———— *Encyclopedia of Victorian Colored Pattern Glass Book 4: Custard Glass from A to Z.* Marietta, Ohio: Antique Publications, 1976.

———— *Encyclopedia of Victorian Colored Pattern Glass Book 5: U.S. Glass from A to Z.* Marietta, Ohio: Antique Publications, 1978.

———— *Fenton Glass: The First Twenty-Five Years.* Marietta, Ohio: O-Val Advertising Corp., 1978.

———— *Fenton Glass: The Second Twenty-Five Years.* Marietta, Ohio: O-Val Advertising Corp., 1980.

Heisey Collectors of America Inc. *Heisey's Glassware.* Reprint of 1915 Catalogue No. 76. Newark, Ohio: 1982.

Innes, Lowell. *Pittsburgh Glass 1797-1891: A History and Guide for Collectors.* Boston, Massachusetts: Houghton Mifflin Company, 1976.

Kamm, Minnie Watson. *Pattern Glass Books,* Volumes 1 to 8 inclusive. Grosse Pointe, Michigan: Kamm Publications, 1939 to 1954.

Lafferty, James R., Sr. *"The Phoenix".* No place: James R. Lafferty, Sr., M.A., 1969

Lechner, Mildred & Ralph. *The World of Salt Shakers.* Paducah, Kentucky: Collector Books, 1976.

Lee, Robert W. *Boston & Sandwich Glass Co. Boston.* 1874 Catalogue reprint. Wellesley Hills, Massachusetts: Lee Publications, 1968.

Lee, Ruth Webb. *Victorian Glass.* Wellesley Hills, Massachusetts: Lee Publications, 1927.

—— *Handbook of Early American Pressed Glass Patterns.* Wellesley Hills, Massachusetts: Lee Publications, 1936.

—— *Early American Pressed Glass.* 36th ed. enlarged and revised. Wellesley Hills, Massachusetts: Lee Publications, 1960.

—— *Sandwich Glass, The History of the Boston & Sandwich Glass Company.* Enlarged and revised. Wellesley Hills, Massachusetts: Lee Publications, 1966.

—— *Antique Fakes and Reproductions.* enlarged and revised. Wellesley Hills, Massachusetts: Lee Publications, 1966.

Lindsey, Bessie M. *American Historical Glass.* Rutland, Vermont: Charles E. Tuttle Company, 1972.

Lucas, Robert Irwin. *Tarentum Pattern Glass.* Tarentum, Pennsylvania: Robert I. Lucas, 1981.

MacLaren, George. *Nova Scotia Glass.* Occasional Paper No. 4, Historical Series No. 1 (Revised). Halifax, Nova Scotia: Nova Scotia Museum, 1968.

MacSwiggan, Amelia E. *Fairy Lamps: Evening's Glow of Yesteryear.* New York: Bonanza Books, 1962.

McDonald, Ann Gilbert. *Evolution of the Night Lamp.* Des Moines, Iowa: Wallace-Homestead Book Co., 1979.

McKearin, George S., and Helen. *American Glass: The Fine Art of Glassmaking in America.* New York: Crown Publishers, Inc. 1971.

McKearin, Helen., and Wilson, Kenneth M. *American Bottles & Flasks: and their ancestry.* New York: Crown Publications, Inc., 1978.

Mehlman, Felice. *Phaidon Guide to Glass.* Englewood Cliffs, New Jersey: Prentice-Hall Inc., 1982.

Metz, Alice Hulet. *Early American Pattern Glass.* 12th Printing. Beverton, Oregon: Charles Metz, 1971.

—— *Much More Early American Pattern Glass, Book II.* Beverton, Oregon: Charles Metz, 1965.

Millard, S.T. *Opaque Glass.* Des Moines, Iowa: Wallace-Homestead Book Co., 1975.

—— *Goblets.* 5th ed. Topeka, Kansas: S.T. Millard, 1947.

—— *Goblets II.* 2nd ed. Topeka, Kansas: S.T. Millard, 1940.

Miller, Everett R., & Addie R. *The New Martinsville Glass Story.* Marietta, Ohio: Richardson Publishing Co., 1972.

Oliver, Elizabeth. *American Antique Glass.* New York: Golden Press, 1977.

Pepper, Adeline. *The Glass Gaffers of New Jersey and their Creations from 1739 to the Present.* New York: Charles Scribner's Sons, 1971.

Peterson, Arthur G. *Glass Patents and Patterns.* De Bary, Florida: A.G. Peterson, 1973.

—— *400 Trademarks on Glass.* De Bary, Florida: A.G. Peterson, 1968.

—— *Glass Salt Shakers.* Des Moines, Iowa: Wallace-Homestead Book Co., 1970.

Pyne Press, The. *Pennsylvania Glassware 1870-1904.* Princeton: 1972.

Revi, Albert Christian. *American Pressed Glass and Figure Bottles.* New York: Thomas Nelson Inc., 1970.

—— *Nineteenth Century Glass: Its Genesis and Development.* Revised ed. New York: Thomas Nelson Inc., 1971.

Rushlight Club, The. *Early Lighting: A Pictorial Guide.* Talcottville, Connecticut: 1972.

Russell, Loris S. *A Heritage of Light: Lamps and Lighting in the Early Canadian Home.* Toronto: University of Toronto Press, 1968.

—— *Lighting the Pioneer Ontario Home.* Toronto: Royal Ontario Museum, 1966.

Sandwich Glass Museum. *The Sandwich Historical Society presents Glass Exhibited in the Sandwich Glass Museum.* Sandwich, Massachusetts: 1969.

Smith, Don E. *Findlay Pattern Glass.* Findlay, Ohio: Privately printed, 1970.

Smith, Frank R. and Ruth E. *Miniature Lamps.* New York: Thomas Nelson & Sons, 1968.

Smith, Ruth E. *Miniature Lamps-II.* Exton, Pennsylvania: Shiffer Publishing Ltd., 1982.

Spillman, Jane Shadel. *The Knopf Collectors' Guide to American Antiques: Glass Tableware, Bowls & Vases.* New York: Alfred A. Knopf, 1982.

—— *American and European Pressed Glass in the Corning Museum of Glass.* Corning, New York: The Corning Museum of Glass, 1981.

Spillman, Jane S., and Farrar, Estelle S. *The Cut and Engraved Glass of Corning: 1868-1940.* Corning New York: The Corning Museum of Glass, 1977.

Stevens, Gerald. *Canadian Glass, c. 1825-1925.* Toronto: The Ryerson Press, 1967.

Stout, Sandra McPhee. *The Complete Book of McKee Glass.* North Kansas City, Missouri: Trojan Press, Inc., 1972.

Sullivan, Audrey G. *A History of Match Safes in the United States.* FT. Lauderdale, Florida: Riverside Press, Inc., 1978.

Swan, Frank H. *Portland Glass.* Des Moines, Iowa: Wallace-Homestead Book Co., 1949.

Thuro, Catherine M.V. *Oil Lamps — The Kerosene Era in North America.* Des Moines, Iowa: Wallace-Homestead Book Co., 1976.

Thwing, Leroy. *Flickering Flames: A History of Domestic Lighting Through the Ages.* Rutland, Vermont: Charles E. Tuttle Company, 1958.

Unit, Doris and Peter. *American and Canadian Goblets.* Peterborough, Ontario: Clock House, 1970.

—— *American and Canadian Goblets,* Vol. 2. Peterborough, Ontario: Clock House, 1974.

Warman, Edwin G. *Milk Glass Addenda.* 2nd ed. Uniontown, Pennsylvania: E.G. Warman Publishing Co., 1959.

Watkins, Lura Woodside. *Cambridge Glass 1818 to 1888: The Story of the New England Glass Company.* New York: Bramhall House, 1930.

Webster, Donald Blake, ed. *The Book of Canadian Antiques.* Toronto: McGraw-Hill Ryerson Limited, 1974.

Wilson, Kenneth M. *New England Glass and Glassmaking.* New York: Thomas Y. Crowell Company, 1972.

—— *Glass in New England.* 2nd ed. Sturbridge, Massachusetts: Old Sturbridge Village, 1969.

Index

Named lamps and patterns are in *italics*

Back cover photograph by Hyla Fox